The Ancient Greeks in Britain

Στον φίλτατό μο[υ]

Λέανδρο Πιπερίδη

με την αγάπη του

Ρένος

Renos Th. Kyriakides

Renos Th. Kyriakides

The Ancient Greeks in Britain

Cyprus 2005

All genuine copies bear the signature of the author.

ISBN: 9963-7619-4-1

1, Andreas Zakos Street, 2404 Nicosia, Cyprus

Tel: +357 22590062

e-mail: renosthkyriakides@yahoo.gr

Printed in Cyprus by L.N.K. Globalprint Services Ltd

This book is dedicated

to the loving memory

of my parents

Themistocles and Olga

who offered me everything.

Aknowledgements

I cordially thank my colleagues,

- Menelaos Christodoulou - *Linguist*
- Theocharis Stavrides - *Historian/Researcher*
- Stelios Nicolaides - *Geologist*
- Demos Christou - *Archaeologist*
- Sofocles Moussoulos
- Leonidas Moussoulos
- Katina Ashikali
- Katerina Stylianou

and Irene Evdokas

for their help in writing this book.

This edition is sponsored by the
Ministry of Education and Culture -
Cultural Services

About the Book

This very interesting and noteworthy monograph by Renos Kyriakides entitled "The Ancient Greeks in Britain" constitutes an additional contribution to the many scientific and popularized historio-archaelogical and philological publications, that deal exclusively with the activities of the Ancient Greeks, and more generally with the Greek life and civilization.

The findings of this laborious research, that took an effort of many years to be completed, show that from the beginning of the Protominoic II period (2300-2100) until the end of the Roman period (395 AD.), and more particularly during the Mycenaean period (1600-1100 B.C.), the southwestern region of Britain was the centerplace from which the ancient Greeks regularly visited in order to extract and transport cassiterite (tin) from Cornwall to Greece. This mineral was non-existent in Greece and was much needed for the making of bronze objects. The same findings also support that the megalithic monument of Stonehenge in the plain of Salisbury, which is related to the prehistoric Greek method of building monuments, was dedicated to the worship of Apollo as well as to his sister

Artemis (Diana) and at same the time, the Greek dodekatheon (the twelve Greek Gods) were generally worshipped in Britain.

The writer, with his hard work, gets all the information and pieces of evidence which he presents in a clear and detailed manner, from a series of writings of Ancient Greek and Latin writers, from reports of contemporary British archaelologists and historians, from a large variety of findings that originate from British archaeological sites, from the cassiterite (tin) reserves of Cornwall and from the various Greek names of islands, cities, rivers, places, headlands and from people from all over Britain.

He tracks and reveals the written depositions of the ancient Greek and Latin writers mainly from the works of Apolodorus, Herodote, Aristoteles, Polivius, Ekataios, Stravon, Diodorus the Sicilian and Plinius, while all the movable findings found in British tombs and other archaeological sites of the bronze age (1500-1100) he collects and studies from writings and theories of famous British archaeologists and historians.

Without exception all the objects that were found in Britain are genuinely of the Mycenaean art, imported directly from Mycenaean Greece or were made in Britain as imitations of the Mycenaean originals, and they underline beyond any doubt, the commercial and cultural relationship between the two countries. These findings in conjunction with the groups of well carved double edged daggers, the pickaxes and the arrow that were carved on the heavy stones of Stonehenge, together with the findings of a similar group of findings at Dorset in the South of England, are, without any doubt, genuine copies of ancient Mycenaean bronze arms and support the positive evidence for the commercial and cultural relationship that existed between Greeks and Britons during the Mycenaean period which went through to the end of the Roman times.

Therefore, the same findings make the conclusions of the author credible, positive, important and irrevocable. In this way this laborious and well presented publication makes it possible to build a vivid interest and to inspire the need for a deeper scientific research and in-depth investigation of the subject for the collection of more information and evidence that are needed for its full substantiation. The publication of this whole work in English and other languages would surely contribute a great deal to the strengthening of this important and very much needed research. Finally, I heartly congratulate the naturalist Renos Kyriakides for his honourable attempt to deal with this important and substantial theme.

Dr. Demos Christou

Former Director of the Cyprus Department of Antiquities

Prologue

Since 1961 I have been teaching in schools of secondary education in Cyprus as a teacher of physics and natural science.

In 1966 I was given a scholarship by the British Council to study the new methods of teaching the natural sciences in Britain.

While was passing by the bookstore of London University I saw the cover of a book entitled "*The growth of civilization*" by G. Field in the window and I went in and bought it. I stood at the corner of the bookstore and skimmed through it. I saw a picture of a certain Monument in the South of England that looked like the Mycenaean Cyclopean Walls and read on page 67 that on a block of stone was carved the Mycenaean dagger and that Mycenaeans may have gone to Britain for tin.

The following Sunday I found myself next to that same stone, at Stonehenge in the valley of Salisbury in the south of England.

I then found myself going through numerous libraries of both London and Oxford, collecting facts about the presence of the Ancient Greeks in Britain.

That is how this study began. For thirty three years I have been digging through books, whether they were in English, Latin, Greek, or Arabic, searching for the numerous signs of the presence or passing of the Ancient Greeks through Britain as well as in the whole world. First I started writing down my findings, then I recollected and consolidated my thoughts and then wrote them down once again.

I was overwhelmed in my effort to get as much as I thought was necessary for the completion of my study.

I have come across tremendous of difficulties in Archaeology, in History, and in the study of Ancient Manuscripts. Many times I had even considered to put an end to my efforts. But how could I? It was a historical challenge I had to respond to.

Introduction

The present study has as a purpose the deposition of all the evidence for the presence of Ancient Greeks in Britain during the age of metal. The evidence is based on the following:

- Geography of British islands in ancient times.
- The Ancient Britons and their way of life.
- Hyperboreans.
- Religion in Ancient Britain.
- Carved daggers and pickaxes, at **Stonehenge** in South England, a dagger and pickaxes in **Dorset** of South England and at other places.
- Items of Greek origin or similar to those found in Britain.
- Tin deposits in **Cornwall** in South-West England and their relationship with Mycenaeans.
- Greek names for areas in Britain, as were found there by the Romans, when they took over the island.
- The relation of Hercules with Bretany and Britain.
- Testimonies of modern English researchers (archaeologists and Historians) of the presence of Ancient Greeks in Britain.

As I have mentioned in my prologue above, this study began in 1966, when I found myself in England, thanks to a scholarship for one year of postgraduate studies on the new methods of teaching natural sciences. I was so enthusiastic with this study that I did not take into account the time or the trouble or expenses necessary for its completion.

Thankfully, I was a professor of natural science so I could easily deal with the Tin deposits of Cornwall, which was the basic reason of the presence of the Ancient Greeks there. I may not be a philologist but I can easily deal with literature. Here I was aided by the fact that I had been a graduate of the Classical Department of the Pancyprian Gymnasium and a good student of the great teacher **Constantinos Spiridakis.**

One of the basic questions that occurred to me was: where did the Mycenaeans find Tin during the Bronze Age. To create Bronze there has to be a mixture of nine (9) parts of Copper and one (1) part Tin.

The Trojan War and The Mycenaean Civilization in general demanded millions of tons of copper and thousands of tons of tin. Where from did the Mycenaeans get such large quantities of Tin? Greece does not have any Tin nor is there any in the surrounding areas. I had to devote a lot of time in the library of the British Museum to find reports of Ancient Greek and Latin Historians and

Geographers who gave me the right answers and helped me follow the correct course to complete this study. It took me overall thirty three years to complete the present study.

Due to my personal problems and pastimes, this study was never shown to the public. I already feel overwhelming satisfaction because I am well convinced that I have completed a historical mission.

CONTENTS

CHAPTER 1

ANCIENT BRITAIN AND BRITONS

Geography of the British Islands in Ancient Times

The first written historical references are those of Pytheas of Marseilles[1] in 335 BC.

He discovered that Britain has triangular shape and that the length of its three sides is 42500 stadia. He also estimated the distance of Britain from the coasts of Europe. He calculated that the shortest distance is at cape Kantio (S.E.Britain), and it is a hundred stadia. Whereas the distance at Cape Velerio from the continent is a four-day sailing. The distance between Velerio and Cantion is 7500 stadia.

He passed by the islands Orkney, Shetland and Faroe and reached the island of Thoule or Thole, present day Iceland.

The same is reported by Timaeus[2]. (Timaeus & Hist, 345-250 BC, Fragmenta, Volume - Jacoby). The Latin writer Fabius Rusticus and Livy, compare the shape of the island of Britain to an elongated diamond or a double-headed axe. As one advances towards the

North, he is confronted with an immense and shapeless country, projecting out to the lands ending in a kind of wedge.

In Scholia of Dionysium[3] we read that, this land of Britain is larger than the other islands which are near it. The other islands are anonymously called Islets.

Tacitus[4] informs us that there is no land opposite its Northern edges, which are washed by wild and open sea. Ptolemy Claudius 108-168 A.D. is the first Geographer, who prepared the map of British Islands. He informed us about the duration of the day in comparison with the duration of the day in Alexandria of Egypt. He also speaks about the parallels and meridians in Britain (p. 82).

Strabo[5], Geography 4, 5, 2 - 3 says that the weather in Britain is very cold, because it lies near the north pole. The weather is more rainy than snowy and on the day of clear sky for prevailing so long a time that throughout a whole day the sun is to be seen for only three or four hours round about mid-day. The greatest part of the island is a plain and it is full of forests, but there are also many hills. It has wheat and pastures and gold and silver and iron.

The same discoveries we read in Diodorus Siculus[6] and Tacitus.

From the above we see, that Geography of Britain was written by the Greek Geographers and Historians. About the Geography of the British Islands speak Pytheas, Diodorus Siculus, Tacitus and Strabo.

1. The course followed by Pytheas

He started in 335 B.C. with Euthymenes (Ευθυμένη) from Massalia. They went through Gibraltar (Pillars of Heracles) and from there Pytheas went north and Euthymenes went south.

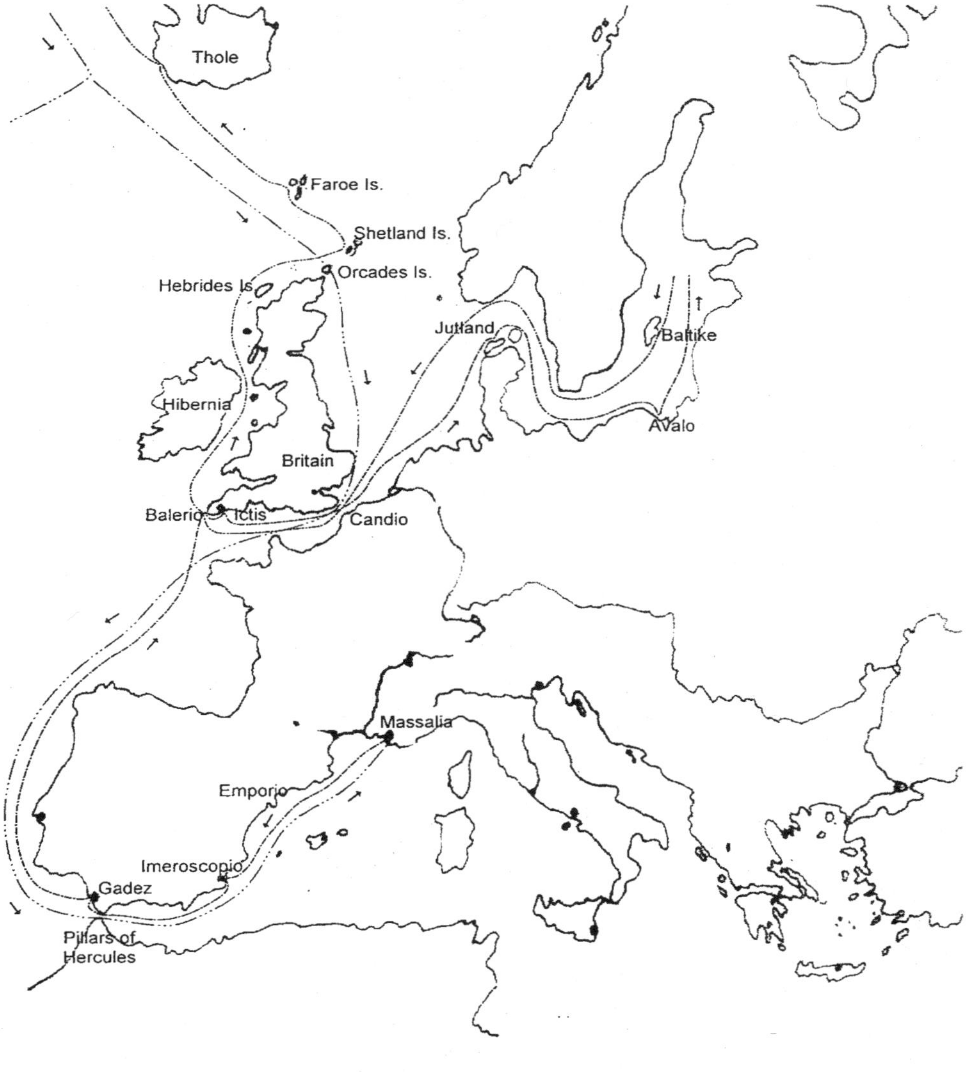

Fig. 1 - The course followed by Pytheas. ***Scale 1:25,000,000***

He followed the ocean coast of Spain and France and reached the South-Western cape of Cornwall which was called Be-Helleri and named it VELLERIO. From Vellerio he continued to the southern shores of Britain. He passed by the island of Iktis to the bay of Penzance and reached the South-Eastern cape of Britain, Kantion. During his course he studied the phenomenon of the tide and connected the flood-tides phases to the moon. The width of the tide in closed bays or where rivers reach the sea surpasses ten meters and one who ignores this fact when approaching the shore may suffer great disasters. If Ceasar had known about it, his fleet would not have been destroyed.

Pytheas even measured the width of the Strait of Dover and found that from Kantion it was one hundred stadia (Attic stadia=177,6m – Olympic stadia=192,77m – Ptolemy stadia=222,22m) and that from Velerio it was a four day sailing journey. The distance between Velerio and Kantion is 7500 stadia.

From Kantion he continued East. He passed Jutland, the place of amber (Ήλεκτρον) and went as far as the Baltic sea. He returned to the South coast of Britain and from Velerio he continued North, between Britain and Ireland–Hibernia (Ιέρνη).

The northern end of Britain he named Orka.

During his course he must have visited the inner parts of the land where he met the inhabitants and their way of life.

He measured the length of the Western coast of Britain and he found it to be 15,000 stadia.

He passed the Orkney islands, he reached the Shetland islands, he went further north to the Faroe islands and went up to Iceland which he named "Thole" island or Thule.

The blurred atmosphere of Iceland is due to the condensation of the gases that emerge from its warm springs and from the gases that also emerge from its hundreds of volcanoes. He called "Thole" the utmost northern British island.

It is situated at a distance of six days' travel from Britain and one day's travel from the ice ocean (πεπηγυΐα θάλασσα - κρόνιο πέλαγος - Υπερβορειο Ωκεανό - Νεκρό Ωκεανό).

These are indications that Pytheas also visited Greenland. This is deduced from the description of the area (Stasonos II, IVI) and also from the fact that at its northwestern shore exists the town of Thole or Thule. During his return he estimated the length of the Eastern coast of Britain which he found to be 20,000 stadia.

Therefore Pytheus is the first great explorer of Britain and Northern Europe, the pioneer of the Greek spirit in those countries.

2. Timaeus in Diodorous Siculus, Book V,21

There are many islands in the ocean, among which the largest is called

Britain. This in the old times was not invaded by foreign forces; because we learn that neither Dionysus nor Hercules nor any of the other heroes or leaders have campaigned against her; in our times, however, Gaius Ceasar, who has been proclaimed god because of his deeds, first among those who are mentioned above has conquered the island, and having vanquished the Britons, has forced them to pay certain taxes. However concerning the latter, we will describe the deeds in detail at the appropriate time, and now we will talk about the island and the tin which is to be found in it.

Because this island is triangular in shape, like Sicily, but its sides are not equal. It stretches alongside Europe, they say that the cape which is the closest to the continent, which they call Kantion, lies up to one hundred stadia from the land, at the place where the sea has an outlet, while they say that the second cape, which is called Velerion, lies four days sailing distance from the continent, and they say that the last one is on the sea, and it is named Orka. The shortest of its sides is seven thousand and five hundred stadia and lies along Europe, the second, from the strait towards the top, is fifteen thousand stadia, and the last one is twenty thousand stadia, so that the total circumference of the island is forty two thousand five hundred stadia.

3. Scholia in Dionysium (Vita-verse of Orbis descriptio 568, line of sholion 3)

As regards their size, they are larger than the other islands. For that reason, the islands, which are near them, he does not call them islands, but, diminutively, islets. The islands of Britain Iouernia (Ivernia) and Alouion (Alvio) are named thus, while the other islands are anonymously called islets.

4. Tacitus

"Britain, which is the largest of the islands known to the Romans, faces Germany on the East and Spain on the West, and Gaul lies on its southern side. There is no land opposite its northern edges, which are washed by wild and open sea. Livy, the best of the older authors, and Fabius Rusticus, the best of the younger ones, compare the shape of the island of Britain to an elongated diamond or a double-headed axe. In fact, this is its shape south of Caledonia, but it is attributed to the whole of the island. However, as one advances towards the North he is confronted with an immense and shapeless country, projecting out to the land's end and ending in a kind of wedge. This shore was first circumnavigated by a Roman fleet which established, in this way, the fact that Britain was an island. At the same time it discovered and occupied the Orkney Islands, which were unknown until that time.

5. Strabo, Geography, 4.5.5

About Thoule, the history is even more vague because of its out of the way position; because from those that we have named it is the northernmost. It is evident from the regions that we know, that the things that Pytheas has said about it and the other places in it are fabrications; because he has falsified most of them, as it has been said before, so that it seems that he is more false about the out of the way regions. As regards, however, the celestial matters and theory of mathematics, it may seem that he used the facts adequately, that those who are near the frozen zone suffer from dearth of cultivated fruits and scarcity of animals, and they feed on millet and other vegetables, fruits and roots.

Galenus (Περι κράσεως και δυνάμεως απλών φαρμάκων. Volume II, p.854 12)

About the moss of Britain

The leaves of the moss of Britain are styptic and adhesive for wounds, just like the leaves of the wild sorrel, but they appear to be darker and fluffier. Their juice is also styptic, so that some, boiling it, consider it the most drastic of oral medications. Because it seems that it heals even those which already start to putrefy.

THE BRITONS

BRITAIN is inhabited by indigenous tribes, who preserve in their customs the old way of life. For they use chariots in their wars, like the ancient Greek heroes in the Trojan War. The island is populous. In their morals they are simple. Their houses are humble, mostly built of straw or wood and they live in the forests. The forests are their cities. They enclose an area with trees after they have shaped a large circle and there they construct huts and keep their flocks. In the harvest they cut off the ears of the grain and store them in roofed granaries. Out of their stock they grind the older ears each day, thus obtaining their food. They are not experienced in gardening and other agricultural matters; although they are rich in milk they do not make any cheese because of their inexperience.

Some of their customs resemble to those of Keltoi*. They are taller than them and less blond and their bodies are softer. During war they mostly use chariots, as some of Keltoi do. They have a lot of similarities to Keltoi.

In Britain there are many kings and leaders and they live mostly in peace with each other. Many men, as well, sleep with one woman and many women prostitute themselves with one man and they hold this illegality as if it was a good law. In Britain strong species of

* Keltoi – Celtic

hunting dogs are fed. Men living along the coast of Okeanos all around the island of Britain are fishermen.

About the Britons we read in Diodorus of Siculus[1], Pytheas[2], Hesiodus[3], Strabo[4], Oppianus[5], Tacitus[6] and Georgious Monachus[7].

1.Diodorus Siculus, Book V, 21

They also say that Britain is inhabited by indigenous tribes, who preserve in their customs the old way of life. That is because they use chariots in their wars, like the ancient Greek heroes in the Trojan War, and their houses are humble, mostly built of straw or wood; moreover, in the harvest they cut off the ears of the grain and store them in roofed granaries; and it is from this stock that they grind each day the older ears, thus obtaining their food; moreover, in their morals they are simple and much different from the shrewdness and cunning people of today. Their diet is also humble and it completely differs from the luxury which results from wealth. The island is populous, and the air there is extremely cold, as if it lies under the Great Bear itself. It has many kings and leaders, and they live mostly in peace with each other.

2. Pytheas

The observations of Pytheas are mentioned by Diodorous from Sicily (Chapter V.20). There live –as they say– in Britain some indigenous

tribes that preserve their old customs and habits, they use chariots at war similar to those used by the Greeks in the Trojan war. Their houses are built from canes and wood. Once they collect their crops they store the wheat in underground storage rooms and every day they take the quantity they need to prepare their food. With reference to their habits they are simple and very different from today's cunning people.
From a point of view of food they are self-restrained and not prosperous. The whole of the island is populated and its weather is cold because it is situated at a very Northern place. It has many kings and leaders that usually live peacefully.

3. Scholia in Hesiodum & Scholia in opera et dies (scholia vet... Prolegomenon scholion sch, page – verse 169 bis, line 13)

Along the coast of Okeanos, which is around the island of Britain, live some men who are fishermen, and are subjects of the Franks, without paying taxes to them. When they sleep around their houses, they hear a voice calling them and feel noise on the doors; when they get up they see some ships, not theirs, full of passengers. Getting inside those ships, by rowing, they immediately reach the island of Britain; although, when they use their own ships, it takes them a whole day with open sails to reach it. When they get there, they disembark the passengers they bring, whom they don't know. Without hearing anyone, they hear the voice of those who welcome them, calling them by name, tribe, kinship and occupation, and the respond in the same way. Thus again immediately, returning to their land, feel the ships lighter.

4. Strabo, Geography, 4.5.2-3

The greatest part of the island is a plain and it is full of forests, but there are also many hills. It has wheat and pastures and gold and silver and iron. These items are taken from the island, as well as hides and slaves, and dogs, which are adept to hunting. The Keltoi, however, use these, as well as the native ones, also in wars. The men are taller than the Keltoi and less blond, and their bodies are softer. An indication of their size is the fact that we saw in Rome adolescents who were taller than the tallest men even by half a foot, even though their legs were not straight nor their form fair. Some of their customs resemble those of the Keltoi, while others are simpler and more barbaric, so that some men who are rich in milk do not make any cheese because of their inexperience; and they are also inexperienced in gardening and other agricultural matters. They also have leaders. In wars they mostly use chariots, as do some of the Keltoi. The forests are their cities; because they enclose with trees that they have cut a large circle and there they construct huts and keep their flocks, not for a long time. The air is more rainy than snowy; while on fair days there is fog for a long time, so that during the whole day one can see the sun for only three or four hours around noon; this also happens to the Morinoi, and to the Menapioi and to all those who are their neighbours.

Caesar the God crossed to the island twice, but has returned quickly, not having done anything great, nor venturing far into the island, because of the revolts that took place among the barbarians, as well as his own soldiers, in the land of the Keltoi, and also because he lost many ships during the full-moon, when there was an increase in the ebb-tides and the flood-tides. However, he defeated two or three times the Britons, although he had with him only two battalions, and carried with him both hostages and slaves and other much booty. Now, however, some of the indigenous leaders, sending envoys and showing good-will, have obtained the friendship of the Caesar; moreover they have dedicated votive offerings to the Capitol, and have turned the entire island almost Roman; they are also submitted to heavy customs duties for the items they export to Keltike and for those they import from there (and these are ivory chains and necklaces and gems and glass utensils and other similar items) so that the island does not need a garrison; because at least a battalion, as well as some cavalry, is needed so that taxes are collected from them, but the expenses needed to support the army would be equal to the money taken from the taxes; because it is necessary to lower the customs duties when taxes are imposed, and at the same time to encounter dangers, when force is used.

5. Oppianus & Epic., Cynegetica, Book 1, line 470 (2ος αι. μ.Χ.)

There is also a strong species of hunting dogs, small in size, but worthy of great renown, which are raised by the wild tribes of the Bretanoi, with the spotted back; to them they gave the nickname "Agassaioi", the frame of whom is similar to the insignificant, greedy, pet dogs, round, lean, hairy, with languid look, but armed with terrifying nails and feet and dense teeth, full of poison; the nose of the Agasseus is superb and he is excellent on the road; because he is very experienced in finding the traces of those who tread the ground.

6. Tacitus

It is not known who the first inhabitants of Britain were, and whether they were natives or have immigrated there from elsewhere, nevertheless they were barbarians. However, their physical traits vary, and this fact alone is suggestive: The red hair and large limbs of the Caledonians show them to be of Germanic origins, while the dark faces of the Silures, their curly hair and their proximity to Spain, lead us to believe that their land has been occupied, in ancient times, by Spaniards. Also, the peoples who are nearest to the Gauls bear a similarity to them. Perhaps the original strain persists, and maybe it is the climatic conditions that determine the physical type in lands, which are the meeting point of peoples living in different directions. However, we may generally estimate that it was the Gauls who occupied the neighbouring island. In both lands one may find the same rituals and religious beliefs. There is no great divergence in language, and there is the same valour in challenging danger, as there is the same cowardice in avoiding it. But the Britons show more spirit, for they have not been softened by extended peace. The Gauls also had their time of military glory, but with peace came decline, and the loss of their liberty cost their bravery. The same fate was reserved for the Britons who have been conquered for a long time, while the rest are still the way the Gauls used to be.

Their strongest point is their infantry. Some of the tribes also use chariots in fighting. The nobleman drives the chariot while his dependants fight and defend him. Once kings ruled them, but now they are torn among the warring factions of rival chieftains. In fact, nothing has hindered them more in war with the strongest tribes, than their inability to co-operate. Very rarely two or three of their tribes unite to confront a common danger: they are conquered as a whole, since they fight isolated. The climate is disagreeable, with frequent rain and mist, but the cold is not extreme. The day is longer than the average in the Roman world, and the night is luminous and short in the extreme North. There is only a short interval between dusk and dawn. If there are no clouds, it is said that the sun's glow may be seen all through the night, for it does not set or rise, but just travels across the horizon. The reason for this must be that the edges of the earth, which are flat, cast low shadows and the darkness doesn't rise at all, which means that the night cannot reach the sky and the stars. The soil is fertile and can produce all kinds of crops, except for the olive, the vine, and other crops, which are native to warmer climates. Crops ripen slowly, but grow rapidly, which is due to the same cause: the extreme moisture of the soil and the atmosphere.

Georgius & Monachus Chronogr., Chronicon breve (lib. 1-6) (redactio recentior), Volume 110, page 81, line 1:

"In Britain many men sleep with one woman and many women prostitute themselves with one man", and they hold this illegality as if it were a good law.

THE HYPERBOREANS

For the case of the Hyperboreans a great lot is written. Some scientific researchers say that they have lived in the Alpes, or beyond them, and researchers believed that they lived in Ripaia Mountains and beyond them. Hecataius and certain others say that beyond the land of the Celtoi, in the north, there lies in the ocean an island. This island is inhabited by the Hyperboreans. The island is fertile and productive of every crop and because of the temperature and the climate conditions it produces two harvests each year. This island cannot be other than Britain. So Britons are Hyperboreans.
The nations of Hyperboreans are three, Epizephyrii, Epiknemidii and Ozolai. They do not eat meat, but they are fed on fruits from the trees. Men of sixty years old are driven away from their city. In general, they respect and apply justice. They cover their bodies with leaves of the plants.
The Hyperboreans worship Apollo. And this, because Leto, his mother was born on this island. The people of the island honour god Apollo exceedingly. And there is a magnificent sacred precinct of Apollo and a notable spherical in shape temple. Offerings were brought from Hyperboreans through Europe to the Adreatic sea. Then to Dodona, where the first Greek people received them

and through Greece to the holy island of Apollo, Delos. On the first journey there were two maidens, Hyperoche and Laodice. On the second journey there were another two maidens, Opis and Arge. Both have Greek names. The Hyperboreans have a peculiar dialect and are mostly friendly disposed towards the Greeks and especially towards the Athenians and the Delians, it seems they have inherited this good will from the most of ancient time. Certain Greeks have visited the Hyperboreans and left behind them the costly votive offerings, leaving inscriptions in Greek letters. And in the same way Abaris, an Hyperborean came to Greece in ancient times and has renewed the good will and kindship of his people to the Delians.

About Hyperboreans we read in Herodotus[1], Hecataius[2], Diodorus Siculus[3], Hellanicus[4], Posidonius[5], Aelius and Herodianus[6], Ioannes Lavrentius[7], and Nicephorus Gregoras[8].

1. Herodotus (Βιβλίο IV, 32-35)

Neither the Scythians, nor the others who inhabit those places do they say anything about the Hyperboreans, except for the Issedones. As I think, they do not say anything either. Because then the Scythians would have said something, as they say about the one-eyed men. But Hesiod has mentioned the Hyperboreans, as did Homer, in Epigonoi, if this epic is truly a work of Homer.

2. Scholia in Apollonium Rhodium & Scholia in Apollonii Rhodii Argonautica (scholia vetera), Page 180, line 8:

Hecataius (73B 4 Diels-Kranz) says that up until his time existed the nation of the Hyperboreans. There are books of his entitled "About the Hyperboreans". The Hyperboreans worship Apollon, that's why he also appeared in the regions beyond. The nations of the Hyperboreans are three, the Epizephyrioi, the Epiknemidioi and the Ozolai.

3. Diodorus Siculus Book II, 47

Now, since we have mentioned the parts of Asia which lie towards the north, we think it is not unbecoming to go through the legends about the Hyperborioi. Hecataeus, one of those who have written the ancient legends, as well as others, say that beyond the Celtic lands, towards the ocean, lies an island which is not smaller than Sicily. This lies towards the north and is inhabited by a people called the Hyperborioi, because they lie further than the north wind. This island is fertile and produces everything, and because of its exceptionally temperate climate, it produces double the crops each year. They say that Leto was born on this island; that is why they honour Apollo above the other gods; and the inhabitants are like priests of Apollo because they daily praise the god with songs continuously and honour him exceptionally. And there is also a magnificent sanctuary of Apollo on the island and an important temple, which is spherical and is adorned with many votive offerings. And there is also a sacred city of this god, most of the inhabitants of which play the cithara, and playing the cithara continuously in the temple they sing hymns to the god, praising his deeds.

The Hyperborioi have their own dialect, and their attitude towards the Greeks is most friendly, and especially towards the Athenians and the Delians, who earned this favour in the older times. And they say that some Greeks visited the Hyperborioi and left luxurious votive offerings written in Greek letters. Similarly, Abaris, one of the Hyperborioi, ended up in Greece in the older times, renewing the favour and kinship to the Delians.

4. Hellanicus Fragmenta, Volume - Jacoby # - F 1a, 4,F, fragment 187C, line 2:

Hellanicus relates that the Hyperboreans live beyond the Ripaia Mountains; also that they are taught not to eat meat, but to feed on fruit from the trees. They drive away from their city the men of sixty.

5. Posidonius Fragment 45, line 2: 44b n - Strabo 4,33

Because of the ignorance about these places, those who tell the tales about the Ripaia Mountains and the Hyperboreans, seem worthy, just like the lies that Pytheas of Massalia told about the land by the ocean, using as a pretext the knowledge about the heavens and mathematics. But let's leave them aside.

Posidonius Fragment 70, line 2: Scholion Apoll. Rhod. 2.675
Herodotus says that the Hyperboreans do not exist at all, because, if the Hyperboreans existed, there would have also existed Hypernotioi. However, Posidonius says that the Hyperboreans exist and that they inhabit the area around the Alps of Italy.

6. Aelius & Herodianus De prodosia catholica, Part+volume 3,1, p.115, line 1:

Hellanicus spells the Hyperboreans with an "ei". Protarchos says that the Alps are named Ripaia Mountains and that all those who live beyond the Alps are called Hyperboreans. Damastis, in his book about the various nations, says that higher than the Scythians live the Issedones, and even higher are the Arimaspoi, and even higher than the Arimaspoi are the Ripaia Mountains, from which blows the North Wind, and that they are never without snow. He says that, even higher than those mountains, live the Hyperboreans, up to the other sea. Kallimachos says the same about them.

7. Joannes Laurentius & Lydus & Hist. De Mensibus, Book 3. Section 1, line 8:

Our own sea, the Mediterranean, takes its water from the Hyperborean Ocean; because it is obvious to everyone that it has two entrances, one in Spain, and the other, as they say, in the Hyperborean Ocean, which the geographers name also Kronion Pelagos, contrary to what Ptolemy believes.

8. Nicephorus Gregoras Historia Romana, Volume 3, p. 511, line 17:

In the twenty eighth chapter of our Roman History, we speak about Russia, which lies near the hyperborean parts of the world.

RELIGION OF ANCIENT BRITONS

The inhabitans of Britain were very religious. This is obvious from many magnificent Temples found in all the reign of Britain. Their deep religious beliefs are tremendously proved by the technique used in building their sacred places. They moved blocks of stones weighing more than twenty six tons covering a distance from 32 km to 321 km. The inhabitants of Britain worshipped the Greek God Apollo, above all others, at important spherical Temples.

It is obvious that the Britons worshipped other gods as well. If we take to account what is mentioned by Strabo, that "the Poseidonian mentions an island near Britain, where religious practice was taking place like those of Samothraki (Greek island), where the goddess Demetra along with her daughter Persefoni" and what Solinus C. Iulius mentions (Collectana Rerum Memorabilium) "Near the warm springs she had her temple, the goddess Athena and in her temple there was always a light", then we can support the idea that, in the country of the Hyperboreans (Britons) the Greek twelve god religion was worshipped.

When Julius Ceasar attacked Northern Europe with his army, he met people who adored the twelve Greek Gods: Hermes, Apollo, Zeus, Athena, Hephaestus and Mars. This is reffered in the memoirs of Julius Ceasar (512) : "All these people adored Hermes more than the others and therefore we can mostly see many places of his worship in Gauls. Apollo, Zeus, Mars and Athena come after in their worship. For the Gauls, Apollo is the only one who treats illness. The Germans believe that Helios and Hephaestus do the same".

Generally, we can say that in North Europe the Twelve Gods' Religion was definitely worshipped. References were made by Herodotus on the subject.

What is written by Herodotus, Hecataius and Diodorus, Siculus and others, is of great importance, because the above mentioned are geographically set and everything mentioned by them is according to History and tradition of that time.

1. It is a fact that the Hyperboreans lived on an island north of France (country of Keltoi). The climate described in the texts is similar to the climate of North France and England.
2. The names Hyperboreans and their three nations, the Epizephyrioi, the Epiknemidioi and the Ozolai are Greek names. Therefore, the Hyperboreans should have been related to the Greeks.
3. They worshipped the Greek God Apollo. They honoured Him as the Greeks did in a circular magnificent temple. That temple can't be other than the glorious circular Temple Stonehenge or any other circular temple from the many found in Britain.

4. The relations between the British Hyperboreans and Greeks were very close. They used to send gifts with Virgins to the main worship place of Apollo at Delos and vise versa, the Greeks were sending their gifts to the Temple of Apollo at Stonehenge.
5. The Geography of Europe and Greece as well, the tribes living in that places, were very well known since that time consequently, the Hecataius reference that Hyperboreans were the inhabitants of Britain must be accepted as being correct.

Herodotus, Book IV, 33-36

33. The Delians say much more about them, saying that offerings wrapped in wheat-straw are brought from the Hyperboreans to the land of the Scythes, and from the land of the Scythes, they are passed on to the neighbours of each land, until they reach to the westernmost limit, on the Adriatic, and from there they are sent to the south, and the Dodoneans are the first of the Greeks to receive them, and from them they come down to the gulf of the Melieans, and cross to Euboea, and from city to city they reach Karystos, and from there Andros is omitted; because the Karystians are the ones who carry them to Tenos, and the Tenians to Delos. And thus these offerings reach Delos. The first time the Hyperboreans sent two virgins to bring the offerings, whom the Delians named Hyperoche and Laodike. At the same time, for the sake of safety, the Hyperboreans sent together with them five of their men as escorts, who are now called Perpherees and have received great honours at Delos. But because those who were sent never came back, the Hyperboreans were discontented that their emissaries did not return, and thus they carry the offerings, wrapped in wheat-straw, to the borders, asking their neighbours to send them on to the other lands. And, sent in this way, the offerings reach Delos. I know myself that there is a similar offering by the Thracian and Paeonian women who, when they sacrifice to Queen Artemis, they present their offerings not without wheat-straw.

34. And I know that they do these. When the two virgins from the Hyperboreans died at Delos, the Delian girls and boys cut their hair; the former before their marriage cut of a lock of hair, wind it around a spindle and lay it on the tomb (and the tomb lies to the left of the Artemisium, under an olive tree), and the boys of the Delians, winding some hair round a blade of grass, lay it also on the tomb.

35. Those virgins, then, enjoy this honour by the inhabitants of Delos. These same also say that Arge and Opis, two other virgins came from the Hyperboreans, through the same peoples, arriving at Delos even before Hyperoche and Laodike. And these two came to bring to

Eileithyia the tribute that they vowed for the easing of childbirth, while they say that Arge and Opis came with the Gods themselves, and they received great honours for themselves; because the women collected gifts for them, calling their names in the hymn created for them by Olen, a Lycian man. It is from them that the islanders and the Ionians learnt to sing hymns to Opis and Arge, calling them and collecting gifts for them (this Olen, coming from Lycia, also composed the other ancient hymns sung in Delos), and when thigh-bones are burnt on the altar, their ashes should be placed on the tomb of Opis and Arge. And their tomb lies behind the Artemisium, turned towards the east, nearest to the refectory of the Keans.

36. And these I have said about the Hyperboreans, because I do not mention the story of Abaris, who was said to be a Hyperborean, and who carried the arrow in the whole earth without eating. But if there are men who are Hyperboreans, there are others who are Hypernotioi. And I laugh seeing that many have already drawn maps of the earth, but none of them has explained it reasonably. Because they draw the Ocean flowing around the earth, which they depict round, as if it was created by a compass, and they show Asia and Europe as equal. Because I, in a few words, will state the size of each and how each of them should be depicted.

CHAPTER 2

THE DAGGER OF STONEHENGE

In the vast valley of Salisbury in the south of Britain lies the Megalithic Monument of Stonehenge. Vast blocks of stone, placed in a circular shape, dominate the green valley, giving to the surrounding calm area a special charm, though raising numerous questions.

Fig. 2 - The Megalithic Monument of Stonehenge

The monument, of religious importance, as many researchers support, was unique in Europe and to the then known world. Taking into consideration that the huge blocks of stones are not from the area of Salisbury, but from areas that are from 20 to 200 miles away, their transfer must have taken place in different times, so the monument must had been for a long time a great religious center, where the people of Britain and of the British Isles used to gather.

The monument has a circular shape, is surrounded by an embankment reaching 5 feet high, which is also surrounded by a ditch with a diameter of around 100 meters. Within the embankment there are in a circle 56 holes, whilst further inside, towards the blocks of stone, there are another two lines of holes, placed in a circle and these are the Y and Z.

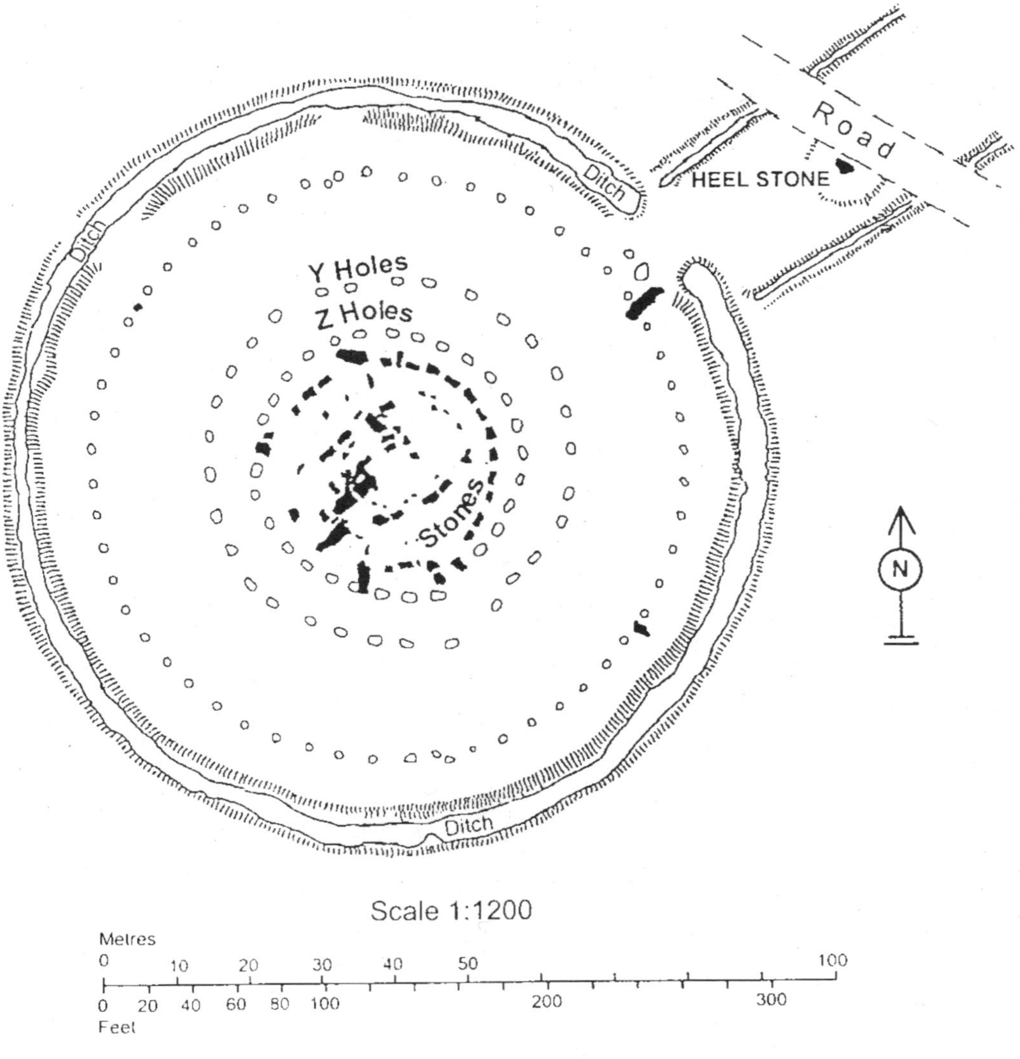

Fig. 3 Stonehenge Plan

The large blocks of some of the monument are classified in two categories: a) in the blocks of stone that are named Sarsens and Lintels and they have been brought from the area of Malborough, which is 20 miles north of Stonehenge, and petrologically they are classified as Sandstones,

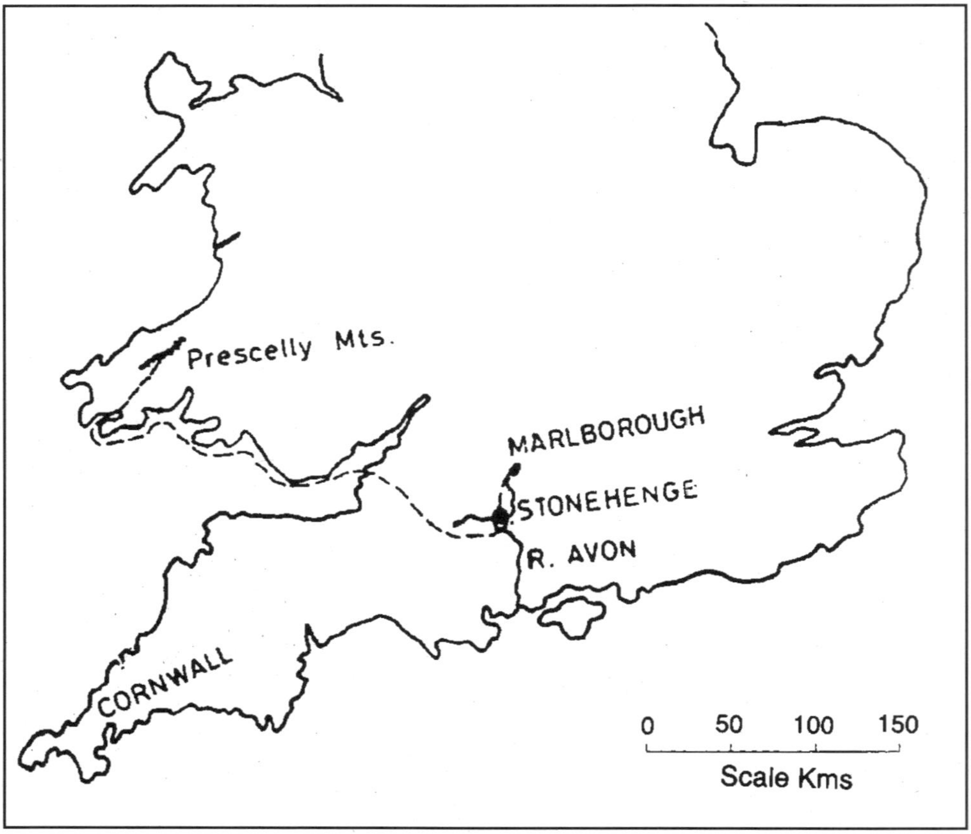

Fig. 4

b) to the blocks of stone that are named Blewstones and have been brought from the mountains Prescelly of Wales, 200 miles north-west. These petrologically are composed of volcanic rock (dolerite).

Fig. 5 Sarsens and Lintels of Stonehenge

The Sarsens, 30 in total, have a height of 14 feet and a weight of 25 tons each. On these there are superimposed another 30 blocks of stone which are called Lintels. Each of them weighs 7 tons. Further inside the circle of the Sarsens, there are 5 Triliths, placed in a horse-shoe shape.

Fig. 6 The author and his children in front of the Trilithons of Stonehenge

On the longest day of the year, the sun rises over the Heel Stone. It stands outside the ditch in the Avenue just by the present-day road. Heel is a greek word for the name of the sun, Helios, Ἥλιος. It is another proof that Stonehenge is dedicated to the god of the sun, Apollo. Entering the horse-shoe shape, we distinguish on the third (from the left) vertical block of stone a complex carving believed to be of Mycenaean type. This complex consists of a dagger with two pick-axes. The dagger has a length of 30 cm with a handle and a blade similar to those found in the Mycenaean tombs and is chronologically placed between 1600-1500 BC.

British archaeologists, who have studied the matter, believe that the dagger of the Monument of Stonehenge was carved at around the same time. During our research in the Stonehenge area, we have

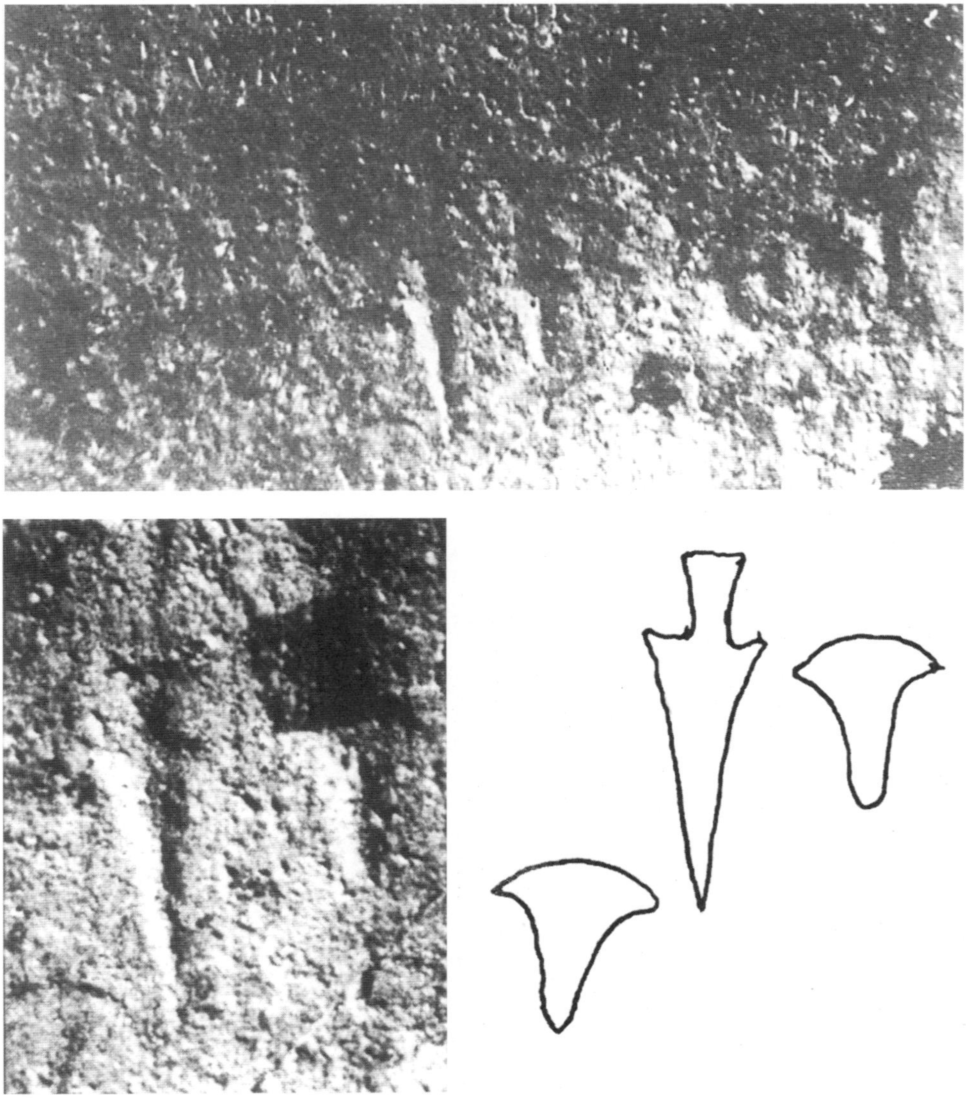

Fig. 7 The carved dagger and the three Mycenaean axes are shown above. A drawing representing the carved items is shown on the right.

noticed a second complex of carved items, which was on the external side of a block of stone (sarsen) of the external circle of the monument. These are composed of two pickaxes identical to those of the Mycenaean dagger complex, and between them there is an arrow. The arrow, as we shall further see is one of the symbols of the God Apollo.

Fig. 8 Carved arrow among pickaxes

Up high on the second standing block of stone of the trilith is carved the male reproductive organ.

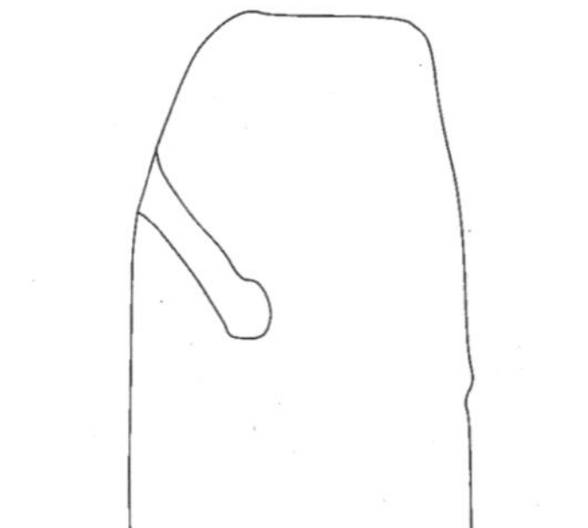

Fig. 9 The male organ carved on the stone, Sarsen 2

We have another carving of the reproductive organ in the house of Falls in Ancient Thera, of Santorini in Greece, built during the classical ages.

Fig. 10 The male organ carved on a stone in Phallos House in Thera, Greece

In Delos of Greece the male reproductive organ is presented by a three meter high stone statue.

Carved daggers and pickaxes have also been found in other areas of Britain. Distinctive is the complex found carved on sandstone slop in Dorset in the south of England. These are of the same type, the same size and of the same timeline as that of Stonehenge.

Fig. 11 Hafted daggers found inside the Barbury Barrow, in Dorset

Many researchers accept the fact that the people who have carved the dagger and the pickaxes on the blocks of stone, must have had some sort of relation to the Mycenaean art.

But when, by whom and for what reason was Stonehenge built? The English historian Atkinson supports the idea that in the valley of Salisbury before 2000 BC. lived people who survived by the hunting they did in the area, "the woods were their towns" according to Stravon. To them land cultivation and the breeding of animals was unknown.

Around 2400 BC. the South England was conquered by European races, who knew of cultivating the land and the breeding of animals, mainly oxen. They lived in houses made of wood and had clothes made of animal skins, their weapons were of stone. These were known as the Wind-mill people.

Around 2400 BC. a new race invaded the British Isles from the shores of Europe, who introduced the custom of burial under rock formations (Dolmen). These people were few in numbers and were those who inserted the art of large bouldered structures, and it is further believed that they are the ones who constructed the first phase of the monument of Stonehenge, the Builders as they are called.

Latest research by Colin Renfew, of Sheffield University establishes the building in a time before 2000 BC. Mike Pitts, in his book HENGEWORLD supports the idea that the Triliths of Stonehenge were placed between 2461-2205 BC. The researcher also believed that the monument of Salisbury Hill belongs to the same time period during which the great pyramids of Egypt were built, that is around 2500 BC. By using the C14 method, a deer's horn found at the base of the block of stone of the trilith, is estimated to belong chronologically to a period of time placed around 2300 BC.

Around 1700 BC. more invaders from the countries of Europe came who knew how to handle clay, how to bake it and make pots. For this reason they were named Beakers. The new invaders brought with them the first copper weapons and golden items and because they had a superior culture they defeated the natives and became rulers of Britain. They reached the mountains of Prescelly in Wales where they discovered the Blewstones and used them in the last phase of the construction of Stonehenge.

Fig. 12 The Bluestones in Prescelly mountain, in Wales

The Beakers later developed trading of metal with people of Europe. About 1500 BC. in the area of Wessex in the south of England appear a race of people with wealth and power. They live during the Bronze Age and the completion of Stonehenge is awarded to them. About the monument of Stonehenge many questions are raised: Was this monument a temple? Which gods did the people who built it worship? What type of ceremonies took place there? By whom was it built and when?

According to the "Stories" of Diodore of Sicily (40-30 BC.) some facts appear on which Hecataius (330 BC.) wrote about the subject. In this island (the British) Lito was born. She was Apollo's and Artemis' Mother. Their father was Zeus. It was when Lito was about to give birth...., and jealous Hera would not allow her to deliver in any country. So Lito was wandering about hopelessly.

Following a command of Zeus, Boreas who drove her to Poseidon, took her near the island of Delos, made a dome of water and with the help of the goddess of Birth Eileithias, who was taken there from Olympus by deceit, gave birth to her twin children, Apollo and Artemis. Apollo, god of the sun and music, was worshipped in Delos, and that is why he was called Apollo the Delian.

Others write that Lito, in order to avoid Hera's rage, escaped to the Hyperboreans.

Those were people who lived to the extreme North, beyond the realm of the god of winds Boreas, and that is where she gave birth to her children.

Others write that Apollo had abandoned Greece to go to the land of the Hyperboreans. That is why Apollo is also called Hyperborean. His symbols were the lyra, the bow and the arrow.

Here in Britain they worshipped Apollo more than any other god. The kings of the city and the leaders of the area were called Boreans because they were descendants of Voreas and the succession to these positions was always a matter of origin. Rob Roy in his book STONE CIRCLES calls Stonehenge a temple.

The circular shape of the monument of Stonehenge and the use of the Lyra as a musical instrument to praise the god, come to show that this was dedicated to the God Apollo.

But the presence of the carved axe shows that Apollo's sister, Artemis, was also worshipped there.

After all these reports Stonehenge cannot be anything but a temple dedicated to the God Apollo.

The second question is related to the book of Rodney Castleden "The Making of Stonehenge". The goddess of Crete Potnia had as a symbol the double axe. Many times the use of double axes was honoured in the name of the goddess, and it was usually presented as the symbol of the goddess. This is the answer to the first and second question.

As for the third question, Hecataius tells us that they continuously praised the god (Apollo) with the Lyra inside the temple and that it was decorated with the believer's offerings.

On the same subject Agricola tells us that during the time he was engaged in his battles, the British were doing ceremonial deeds. "At a time usually devoted to pageantry and ceremonial visits".

Supporting evidence that the temple was dedicated to Apollo is also mentioned in Herodotus' book that two Northern daughters, Argi and Ottis and then another two, Hyperoche and Laodiki (Greek names) started off from their northern country, accompanied by five men and arrived to the island of Delos, the birthplace of their gods, Apollo and Artemis.

As for the fourth question, much was written.

We shall base ourselves on the following elements:

1. On the carved dagger and the axes.
2. On the carved arrow with the axes.
3. The architecture of the monument.

For the first element we mention that almost everybody who wrote about it, admits that is a Mycenaean knife or of a similar type. As for the second, looking at the arrow, this is a symbol of the god Apollo, carved on a block of stone on the monument.

If we take into account the report from Hecataius, that the temple was decorated with the offering of the believers and that they continuously praised the god with the lyra within the temple, we should accept that there was a covered place where the believers could be sheltered from the adverse weather conditions.

So there must have been a place around the blocks of stones that was covered. At the 56 holes outwardly, as the others inwardly, there must have been wooden support poles supporting the covered temple. With reference to the third, I would like to mention what Professor R.J.C. Atkinson wrote, who is a specialist researcher of the subject. "The special details of the way that the Sarsen are placed are so unusual for British standards of that time, so that it is difficult to accept that this way was discovered by the British. If the daggers are indeed Greek, then we can say that the man who designed the Monument of Stonehenge is related to the prehistoric Greek way of building Monuments.

Fig. 13 The way that the stones are joined together. 1. Hole in the underside of the lintel. 2. Projecting knob on the top of Sarsen

The answer to the question as to when it was built, is based on two elements. The first is a piece of wood found in the base of a block of stone of Stonehenge. Its age was found by using the C14 method, to have been in use for a monument that was built before 2000 BC. The second element is the finding of the age of a deer's horn found at the base of trilith dated around 2300 BC.

Based on the facts above we can support the arguement that the monument of Stonehenge had begun being built before 2000 BC.

In a pit within the surrounding ditch in 1978 a human skeleton was discovered. It was proposed that it was a member of the Beakers (1100 - 1500 B.C.). On the skeleton's chest three arrowheads were found which were made of pyritolithos.

This is the only human skeleton that was found at Stonehenge.

There are hundreds of Megalithic stone circle constructions in Great Britain and Ireland. Some of them are found at:

* Stonehenge
* Stennes and Maes Howe - Orkney Inlands
* The ring of Brodgar
* The Avebury Stone Circle
* Castlerigg in Scotland
* Stanton Drew in Somerset
* The Circle At Log End - in West Chazy
* Callanish in Scotland
* Druids Temple in Yorkshire

THE DRUIDS

The inhabitans of France, the Galatians, had close relationship with the Greeks of Marseilles. The Galatian priests "Soumani" learnt from the Greeks the writing and reading of the Greek language. They were initiated in and embrased the mysteries of the worship of Dionysus. The Galatians also accepted the symbol of "Dris", so their priests were called Druids, whereas "Dris" is a Greek word for oak. In French the name of Oak is "Chene" and the forest with oaks is "Gland". In Greece the "Dryads" were the nymphs who had been living in woodlands.

THE KERNOS

A construction similar to the monument of Stonehenge but smaller in dimensions was found in Greece at the palace of Mallia in Crete. It is a circular altar called "KERNOS" with a central hole surrounded all around in its periphery by 34 smaller holes. In these holes the Greeks used to place products (usually agricultural crops) of their first harvest, called "απαρχαί" (the primal crops). This altar – KERNOS– was built probably around 1500 BC.

Fig. 14 kernos

PARALLEL HISTORICAL PERIODS IN GREECE

Periods	Greece Mainland	Cyclades	Crete
Late Bronze Age 1600-1100 B.C.	Creto-Mycenaean Civilization		
Middle Bronze Age 1900-1600 B.C.	Mid-Helladic Civilization	Mid-Cycladic Civilization	Late Minoan Civilization Middle Minoan Civilization 1900-1700 B.C.
Early Bronze Age 2800-2700-1600 B.C.	Early Helladic Civilization	Early Cycladic Civilization	Early Minoan Civilization

HISTORICAL PERIODS IN BRITAIN

Periods	Civilizations	Monuments
1100 Bronze 1500 Age	Wessex Beakers	Salisbury Hill Stonehenge III
1600 Copper 1800 Age		Stonehenge II
1900 Early Neolithic Period	Builders	Stonehenge I
1500 Mesolithic Period	Windmill Hill people	Long Barrows Salisbury Hill
2700-2800	Natives and Hunters	

Fig. 15

CHAPTER 3

ITEMS OF MYCENAEAN ORIGIN

a. The Sword of Pelynt

During the excavations of 1930-1945 in the graveyard near Pelynt of South Cornwall, along with two other swords found, there was a third one which is of Mycenaean type. It is 4 $^{1}/_{4}$ inches long and is in the Truro museum of Cornwall. Professor Gordon Childe believes that the sword was made in the islands of the Aegean Sea around 1400 BC. Similar swords were found in tombs of Kefalinia. But those are dated back to around 1200 BC.

Fig. 16 Bronze sword of Pelynt, South Cornwall was imported from Greece in the thirteenth century BC. Now in Truro Museum.

The archaeologist Aileen Fox, in her book "South West England", also, considers that the above sword is of great importance, because its existence helps to strengthen the belief of British archaeologists who consider that the sword carved on the Stonehenge blocks of stones is of Mycenaean type; in other words, it is the kind of sword found in Mycenaea during 1600 B.C. Both facts convince that residents of Greece had dealings with the residents of the British Isles and show the presence of Greeks - Mycenaeans in Britain.

b. The Golden Cup of Rillaton

In the area of Rillaton in Cornwall, in late 1818, a tomb was discovered with very rich archaeological findings.

Fig. 17 Golden cup from Rillaton, East Cornwall. It was found in 1818. The form is derived from gold cups in the shaft graves at Mycenae.

The most impressive of those is a golden goblet. It is $3^1/_3$ inches long and has horizontal stripes and a strip type handle. Its technical fabrication is almost identical to the fabrications of the metal technicians in Greece, because similar goblets were found in the Mycenaean tombs and are dated around 1600 BC. They are now in the British Museum.

c. The Sceptre of Salisbury

In the plains of Salisbury of South England was discovered a tomb of a warrior with a scepter inside. On its recess are fixed added pieces of bones ornamented in a broken line design. According to the view of Professor Piggot a similar scepter was found in a pothole type tomb in Mycenae and is dated around 1600 BC. (See Piggot, Ancient Europe, page 134).

Fig. 18 - Sword of Santorini -1500 BC.

The art of adding valuable materials on metal objects appears to have been perfected in the Greek realms as witnessed by a sword found in Santorini (dated before 1500 b.c.) and many other similar objects which were found in tombs in Mycenae

Fig. 19 - Sword of Mycenae

d. The Hameldon Dagger

At Hameldon place in Dartmoor, the cremation with a grooved dagger decorated with gold pins was found under a slab pavement. Its decoration shows that it is copy of Early Bronze Age weapon of the eastern Mediterranean.

e. The double axe of TOPSHAM

Near Topsham of South Britain, was discovered a double axe which is now in the British Museum in London. It is about 5 inches long, with an egg-shaped hole in the middle and is made 94% of copper.

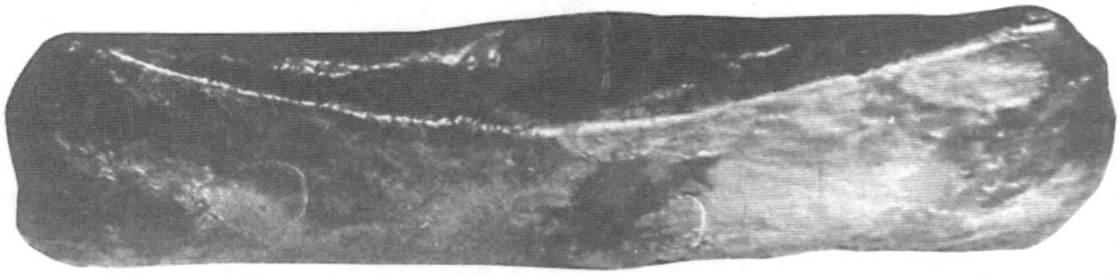

Fig. 20 - The double axe of Topsham, copper double axe that was found in Topsham Devon.

It was imported from the Aegean (1300 - 1200 BC.)
Without a doubt this axe was made in an island of the Aegean sea. Similar axes were found in the Acropolis of Athens and in Mycenae and are believed they have been made and used in the middle of the 13th century BC.

f. The Tin Ingot

The ingot from the Fal estuary, St. Mawes Cornwall. Shaped to an astragalus, easy handling for transportation. This ingot is an evidence for export of Cornish tin in other countries. Length 2 feet 10 in. Weight 158 lbs. Now is in Truro Museum.

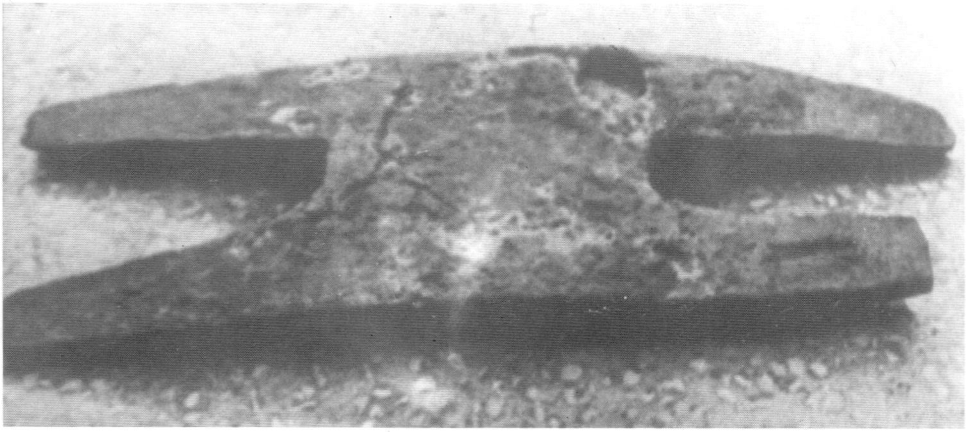

Fig. 21 - Ingot of tin in the shape of an astragalus found in Cornwall

g. Silver coin of Alexander III of Macedonia

In Penzance of South Cornwall 43 silver drachmas which are identical to those made in Marseilles in the 2nd century B.C. were found. A Greek silver coin from Holne, near Bukfast, is evidence of the presence of Greeks in ancient Britain.

Fig. 22- Actual size of a Greek silver four-drachma coin with the head of Alexander III of Macedonia (326 BC.) All in the museum of Torquay in Cornwall.

Surely, it would be possible, that Britons or other people of Northern Europe visited Greece and carried with them Greek objects on their way to their country. But there is no evidence of any visit of Britons in Greece. It is true that Herodotus (484-411 BC.) tells about virgins' visit to Greece from the far North (Book IV, 33). But virgins from the far North died and were buried in Delos. However, from the written evidence of ancient writers, which we present below, and according to the opinion of British contemporary specialists presented towards the end of this study, we rather decline to accept the first opinion, that is: Greeks visited Britain. But why did Mycenaeans, Cretes and generally people of the Greek realm visit the British islands?

h. Jewels of Mycenaean Art

Other evidence of the existence of a close relationship between Mycenaeans and the inhabitants of Britain, is the large number of jewels that were found there and which were carrying a Mycenaean artistic style, like beads of amber and others which, as shown on map (fig. 23) were found in almost all places of Britain. Their presence in this area reveals the contact Greeks had with the British and the further influence of the Greeks upon the British.

The connection between the Aegean world and the British islands that began during the prehistoric ages, continued through to the historic times as proved by the above findings. In an artificial cave near Teighmouth two goblets from Attica and a wine cup of the 4th century BC. came to light after excavations, which can be seen today in the Museum of Torquay. In Holne of Cornwall near Bukfast, a farmer found a silver coin with the head of Alexander the Great.

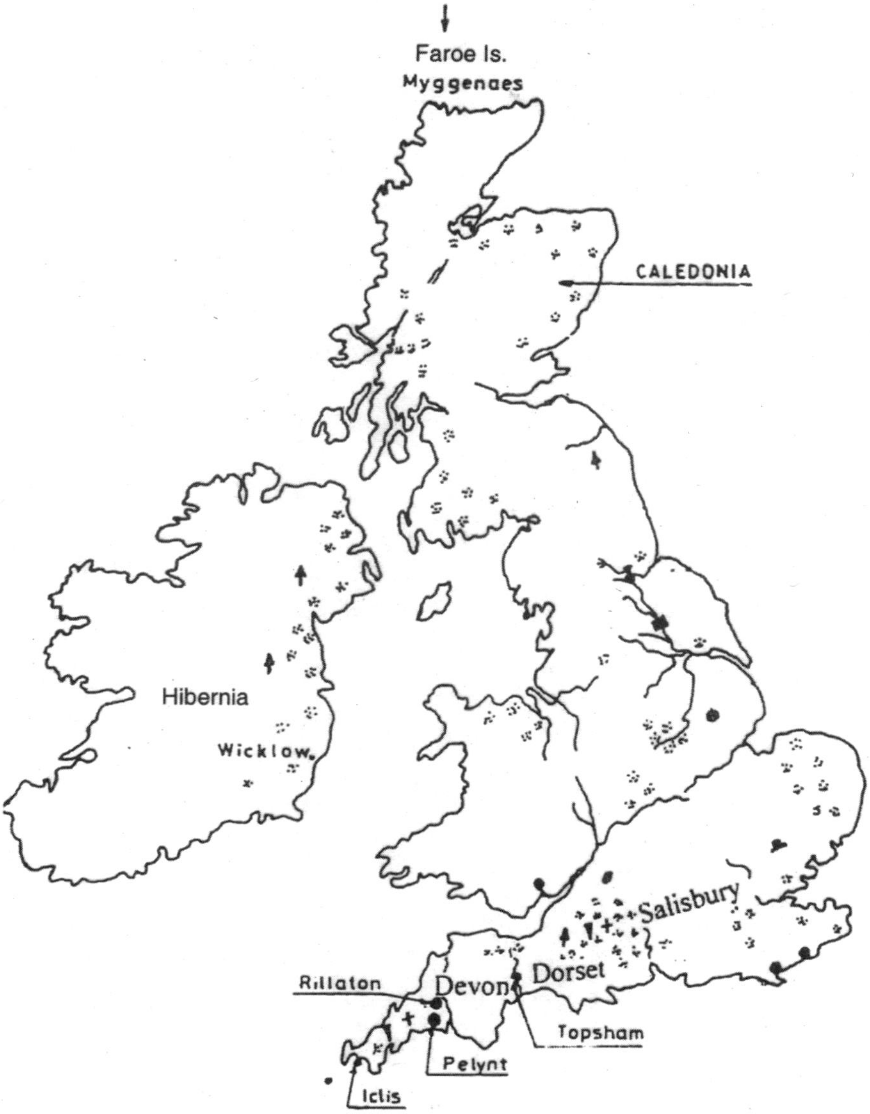

Fig. 23 - A map of Britain and Ireland comparatively, with marked points of the places through which ancient Greeks and other visitors passed and left their traces.

Beads of amber • Objects decorated with bones

+ Areas where metals were processed Axes and double axes

The Travels of Pytheas

Pytheas was born around 370 BC. in Marseilles (Μασσαλία) from Greek parents. Marseilles (Μασσαλία) was built by the Phocaens (Φωκαείς) towards the end of the 7th century in the Mediterranean coast of France. Pytheas was a Geographer, Mathematician and Astronomer and around 335 BC. he travelled to Britain and Northern Europe.

His travel expenses were undertaken by the Lords of Massalia often called Timouchi (Τιμούχοι) or even by Alexander the Great. These views are supported by the fact that he disclosed his geographical findings which he had never published to the Timouchi. The view that he might have been sent by Alexander the Great is supported by the fact that in the places visited by Pytheas were found silver coins of Alexander the Great (Figure 22). At that time, the Carthaginians (Καρχηδόνιοι) seemed to be worried about Alexander's intentions to the west and they had sent to Babylon a representative called Halmikar to find out whether Alexander the Great had programmed a military campaign to the west upon the completion of the one to the East.

It is possible that Pytheas's exploratory travels had something to do with Alexander the Great. It is also known that together with Pytheas Euthymenes (Ευθυμένης) had also began an exploratory voyage to West Africa. All travel explorations of Pytheas were written by him in a treatise entitled "Γης Περίοδος η Περί Ωκεανού" (translated as about the Earth and Oceans).

TACITUS ON BRITAIN

Tacitus was a friend of Pliny the Younger and married the daughter of Agricola.

He wrote about his father-in-law in the book "On Britain and Germany", where he mentions the history of Agricola's actions.

Agricola campaigned seven times against the Britons and was appointed by Rome as Governor of Britain. The first campaign was in AD 77 and the last one in AD 84.

The Romans wanted to conquer Britain, because it was said that it had gold, silver and other metals. (Tacitus does not mention tin).

** Tacitus mentions that in Britain there were "small and great states".*

** "It was felt that for a man to tell the story of his life showed self-confidence and not arrogance".*

** Britain was a dangerous place for the Romans, so Tacitus said that "We were forced to fight for our lives before thinking about victory"*

In Britain, also, are to be found gold, silver and other metals, which make it worthy to be conquered. In the ocean are also to be found pearls, which are, however, dark and dotted. Some consider the natives unskilled in collecting them. While in the Red Sea the oysters are collected from the rocks, while they live and breathe, in Britain they are collected when they are washed up from the sea. It is easier to believe in the defect of the quality of their pearls, than of human greed.

* *"Once each tribe was ruled by its own king".*

* *"We are fighting to protect our land, our wives and our parents, while the Romans are fighting due to their greed and softness".*

* *"The Gods are finally showing clemency to us the Britons, by keeping the Roman general with his army away from us, exiled in another island".*

* *Led by such encouragement, the entire island rose under the leadership of Boudicca, a woman of royal descent (the Britons do not distinguish sex in their leaders). They attacked the Roman troops in their scattered posts, raided the garrisons and besieged the colony itself, which they considered the cause of their slavery. And the furious victors did not refrain from committing any form of savagery and cruelty.*

* *He conquered by force the strong and bellicose tribe of the Silures, having to overcome not only a valiant enemy, but also a perilous terrain.*

* *At the time of his first entry into the province, a time usually reserved for ceremonies and official visits, did he not deliberately choose a difficult and perilous enterprise?*

* *He chose himself the sites for the camps, personally inspecting rivers and forests, and he gave the enemy no rest, launching relentlessly raids for plunder.*

* *Agricola officially assisted in the construction of temples, public squares and private mansions.*

* *Some relate that he could be very harsh in punishment, and he was*

as harsh to the wrongdoer, as he was benevolent to the right-doer.

** Since he was afraid of a general rising of the northern tribes and of the threatening moves of the enemy on land, he used his navy to inspect the harbours.*

** When the adversaries learnt of this, they suddenly changed their plan and prepared for a night raid on the ninth legion, which seemed to them to be the weakest point. They created panic into the sleeping camp, killing the sentries and breaking into it.*

** A leader of the Caledonians, named Calgacus, addressed the 30,000 men summoned for battle, with the following words: "... We instinctively love our children and our family above all else, but they are taken from us by conscription, to serve in other lands. Our Roman enemies when they do not rape our wives and daughters seduce them, appearing to them as guests or friends. Our properties and possessions are taken as tribute, our land and its produce is taken to supply corn, our bodies and hands are taken to construct roads through forests and marshes, and all that with violence and insults" ... "The Brigantes, led by just a woman, burned the colony, assaulted the garrison and, if they hadn't become intoxicated by success, could have cast off the yoke. So, as we are uncorrupted and unconquered, let's prepare to fight for freedom, without fearing defeat, proving from the first battle, what heroes are raised in Caledonia."*

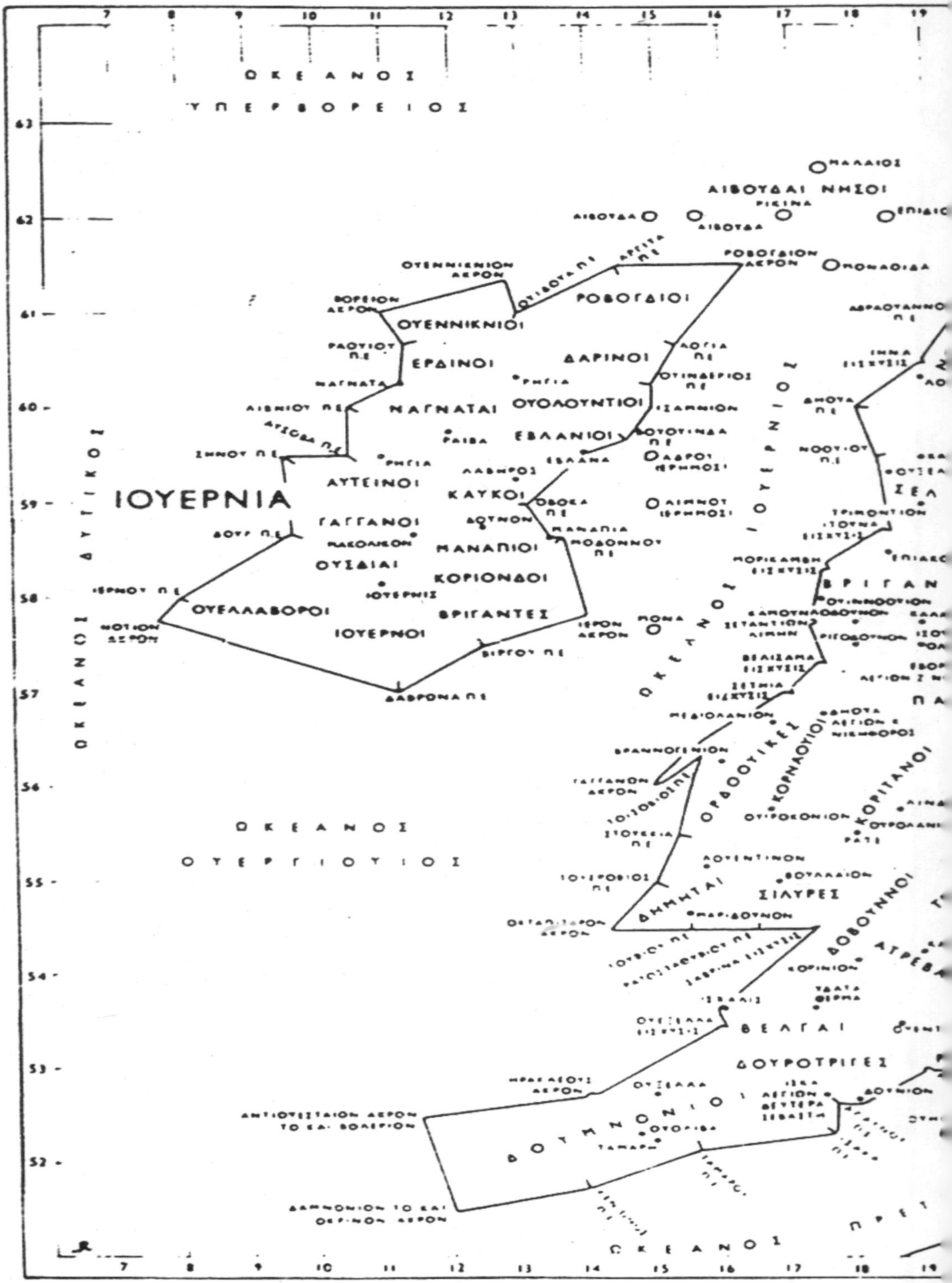

Fig. 24. - Map of Claudius Ptolemaeus from Alexandria

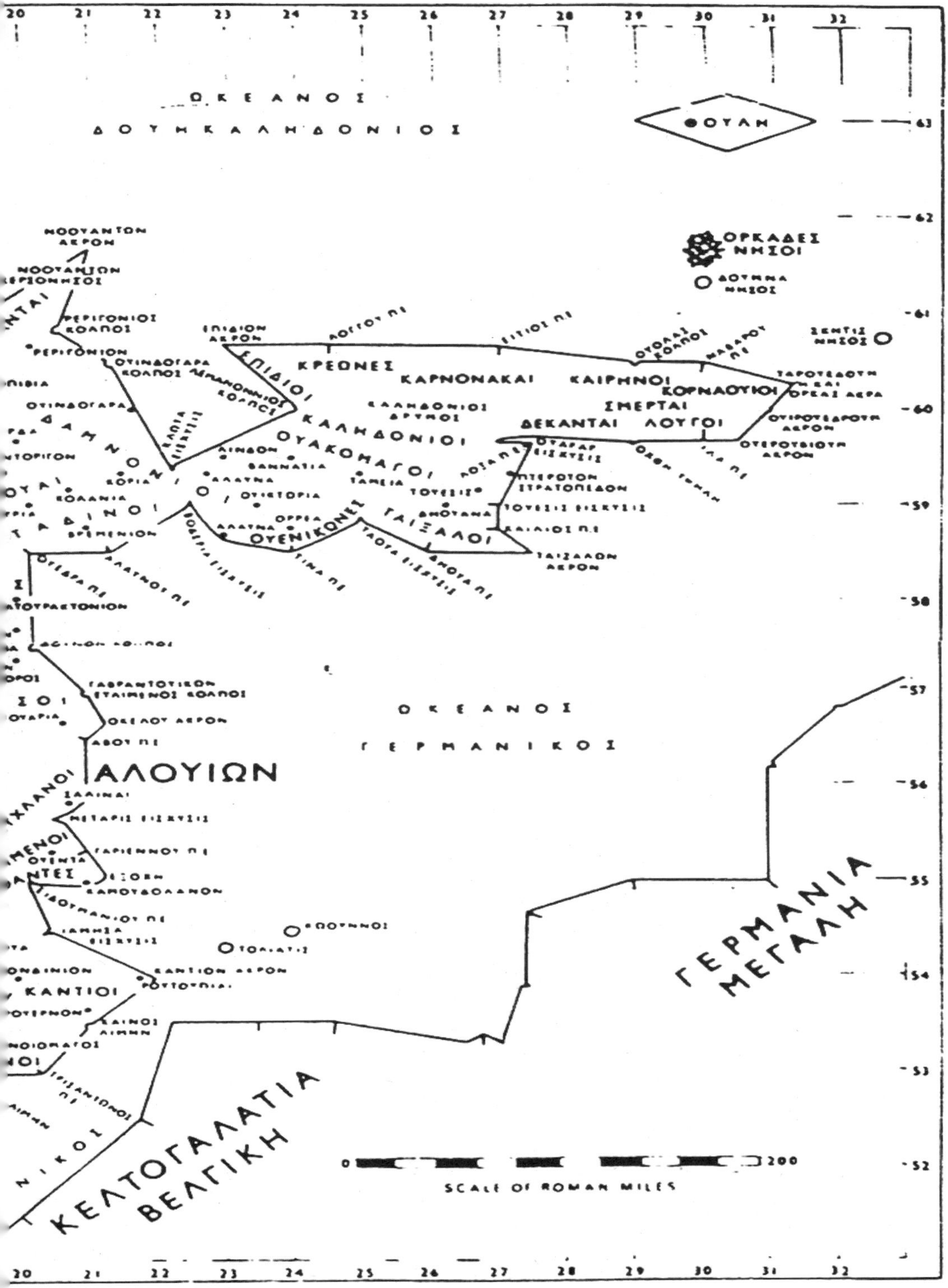
ΩΚΕΑΝΟΣ
ΔΟΥΗΚΑΛΗΔΟΝΙΟΣ
ΘΟΥΛΗ
ΟΡΚΑΔΕΣ ΝΗΣΟΙ
ΕΠΙΔΙΟΙ
ΚΡΕΩΝΕΣ
ΚΑΡΝΟΝΑΚΑΙ
ΚΑΙΡΗΝΟΙ
ΚΟΡΝΑΟΥΙΟΙ
ΣΜΕΡΤΑΙ
ΔΕΚΑΝΤΑΙ
ΛΟΥΓΟΙ
ΚΑΛΗΔΟΝΙΟΙ
ΟΥΑΚΟΜΑΓΟΙ
ΟΥΕΝΙΚΩΝΕΣ
ΤΑΙΞΑΛΟΙ
ΩΚΕΑΝΟΣ
ΓΕΡΜΑΝΙΚΟΣ
ΑΛΟΥΙΩΝ
ΚΑΝΤΙΟΙ
ΓΕΡΜΑΝΙΑ
ΜΕΓΑΛΗ
ΚΕΛΤΟΓΑΛΑΤΙΑ
ΒΕΛΓΙΚΗ
0
200
SCALE OF ROMAN MILES

PTOLEMY CLAUDIUS - GEOGRAPHER (108-168 A.D.)

The Beginning of Europe. First Map

The first map of Europe contains the British Islands, together with the islands around them. The parallel, which runs through the middle of this map, as to the meridian latitude, has a ratio of about eleven to twenty.

The map is surrounded on all sides by ocean. On the east by the ΓΕΡΜΑΝΙΚΟΣ, on the south by the ΠΡΕΤΤΑΝΙΚΟΣ and the one called ΟΥΕΡΚΙΟΝΙΟΣ. On the west lies the ΔΥΤΙΚΟΣ and on the north we find the ΥΠΕΡΒΟΡΕΙΟΣ and the one called ΔΟΥΜΚΑΛΗΔΟΝΙΟΣ.

And the island of Thoule, on the longest day has twenty equatorial days, and it differs from the hours of Alexandria two hours and five to the west. It has eleven and fifty eight degrees.

The official cities of the island of Iouernia. Iouernia, the city homonymous to the island, has eighteen hours on the longest day and differs from Alexandria three and a quarter hours to the west.

Raiba, has eighteen and a half hours on the longest day and differs from Alexandria three hours and five to the west. And in the island of Alouion, Londinion has eighteen hours on the longest day and differs from Alexandria two hours and a third to the west.

And the Winged Camp (Pteroton Stratopedon) has nineteen hours on the longest day and differs from Alexandria two hours to the west. And the island of Arktis has sixteen hours and one third on the longest day and differs from Alexandria two hours and one third to the west.

CHAPTER 4

TIN DEPOSITS OF CORNWALL

Tin is an element that is found in igneous rocks with a content of 0.001‰. The main mineral of tin is tinstone, a mineral of magmatic origin and the product of the following chemical reaction:

SnO_2 +2C (1200°C - 1300°C) ➔ Sn +2CO

It is directly linked with tin-bearing pegmatites that are associated with acidic granitic magmas. The tin deposits of Cornwall are directly associated with the granitic rocks of the region (Figure 25).

In the granitic mass there are veins, within which tin is observed; tin is also associated with small quantities of Ag- and Pb-bearing minerals. In the same area there are cupriferous deposits that are associated with metamorphic rocks. Along with these minerals there are Fe-bearing minerals that form the Dartmoor deposits.

People exploited tin in the past, either from the granitic veins or from stream sediments as a product of erosion.

It has been observed from that time that if a small amount of tin is mixed with copper then a hard and durable alloy is formed, known as bronze (bronze is an alloy of copper and Sn or bronze is an alloy of copper and zinc).

Apart from these two elements (Zn and Sn), copper alloys were produced containing Pb, As, Ni, P and other elements. Native, As-bearing brass was found in cupriferous deposits of Caucasus and in the Talmezi deposit of Iran.

In Cyprus there are cupriferous deposits containing As in the Limassol Forest region. It is worth noting that in the Faneromeni area (Episkopi, Limassol), copper items have been found with high As content, that is arsenic-bearing bronze).

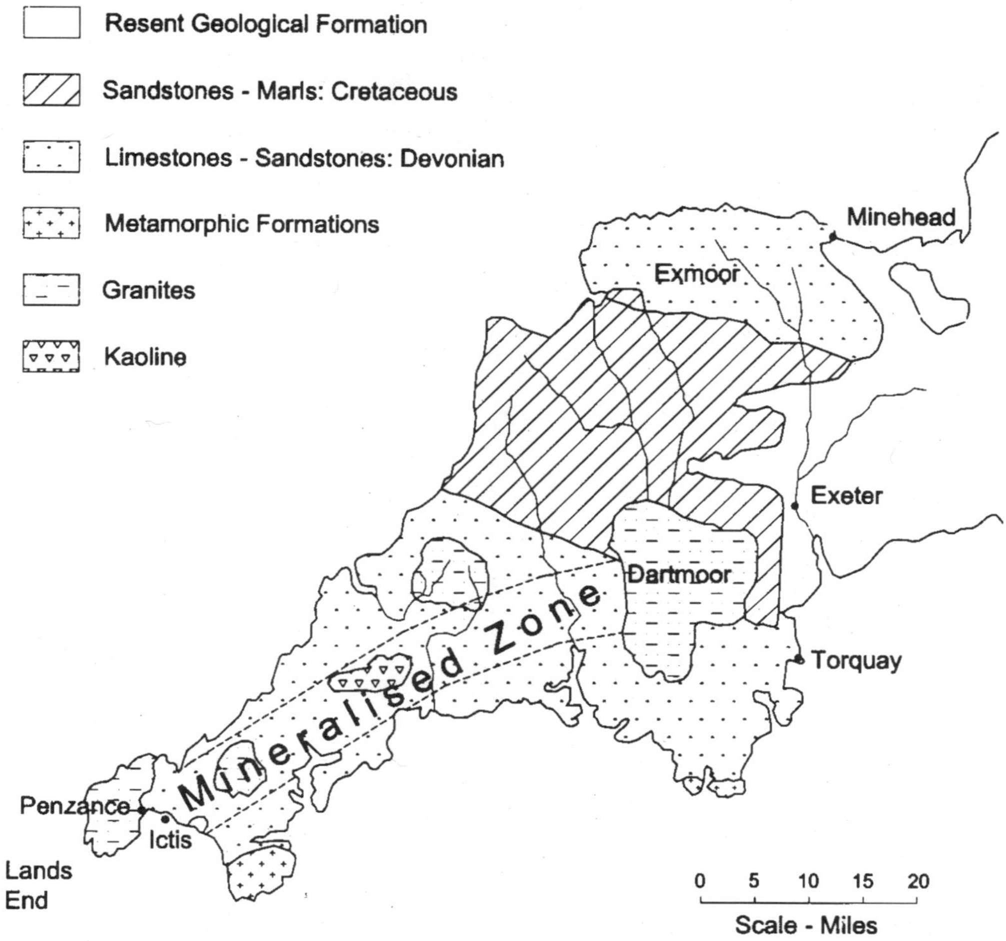

Fig. 25 - Geological map of Cornwall

The first people who used bronze were those who lived near Mesopotamia. Then people from the Mediterranean and later from Europe followed. This is based on the discovery of bronze items in these regions. Analyses of items from Mesopotamia (4000 BC) revealed that they were made of 85% Cu and 15% Sn. In Anatolia and

Caucasus tin was used around 2000 BC (Jessen - Antiquity, vol. 12, 1938, p. 341-345).

Depending on the use of bronze, alloys with different portion of Cu and Sn were made. The more tin used in the alloy the harder the alloy. Bronze used for manufacturing weapons had 16 parts Cu and one part Sn. For stronger weapons the ratio of Cu to Sn was 7:1, whereas for statues the ratio was 9:1 (with the addition of Zn and Pb). For the making of coins, 9.5 parts of Cu and 0.5 parts of Sn and Zn were used.

An important benefit of the addition of As and/or Sn in the alloy is that both elements act as fluxes, reducing the melting point, and the solidification of the melt takes longer, thus producing smoother surfaces avoiding the formation of bubbles.

Ancient Greek and Roman geographers, historians, and philosophers made reference to tin in their writings. In the ancient Greek epic Iliad written by Homer, there is a description of the making of the breastplate that Kiniras from Paphos gave to Agamemnon. Homer also mentions (p. 474-475) that Volcan (God Hephaestus) threw in the fire copper (unprocessed), tin, precious gold and silver.

Homer, Iliad, Book XI

And the son of Atreus shouted that the Argives should prepare for battle, and he himself was girded with bronze. He first put on beautiful greaves, with silver ankle-pieces around his legs; then he put around his chest the breast-plate, which was given to him as a gift at one time by Kinyras. Because he had heard in Cyprus the great glory, that the Achaeans were preparing to sail to Troy in their ships; and because of that he gave the king that gift. On that there were ten bands of black cyanus, twelve of gold and twenty of tin; and dragons of cyanus winded up, three on each side, like rainbows that the son of Kronos had fixed on the clouds, a monster for mortal men. And on both sides of his shoulders he placed his sword, whose golden nails shone, and his sheath was silver, with chains of gold. And he grabbed his beautiful ornamented shield, around which there were ten circles of gold, and on which there were twenty navels of white tin, and in the middle there was one of black cyanus.

Homer, Iliad, Book XVIII

And the bellows, twenty in number, were blowing in the furnaces, emitting every kind of strong wind, sometimes helping him immediately, as if he was in a hurry, sometimes in whatever way Hephaistos wished, in order to further his task; and in the fire he put unbending bronze and tin and precious gold and silver; and then he placed a great anvil and he took on one hand a steady hammer and tongs on the other.

In the above-mentioned paragraphs Homer reveals that tin was used as ornamental stone as well as for the manufacture of alloys. However, there is no mention for its provenance, a fact that constitutes a significant omission taking into consideration that there are no known tin deposits in Greece or in neighbouring areas.
Plato in "Critias" (116.B) describing the buildings of Atlantis writes:
Aristotle in "Meteorological" (388 a 14 and 389 ab) refers to tin as the most known metal and parallels its properties with those of other metals.

Plato, Critias

And the entire circumference of the wall of the outer circle they covered with copper, just like plaster, while that of the inner circle they covered with tin, and the one around the acropolis, with bronze, with fire-like sparkles.

Around 1st century BC, geographers and historians such as Pliny, Diodorus of Sicily, Strabo, Timeus (346-250 BC), and Posidonius (135-51 BC) inform us with considerable details not only about the metal's provenance, but also about the way of its transportation to

Greece. We are informed from Pliny's book "Natural History" (Chapter XXXIV, 156-157) that there were the areas of tin along the Atlantic Ocean:

1) Northwest of the Iberian Peninsula, today's Spanish areas of Orense and Zamorra, as well as the Portuguese areas of Beira, Mincho and Tros-o-Montes.
2) In central France and the area South Breton along the Atlantic shores.
3) In Cornwall and southwestern Britain.

Also, there are references in ancient scripts about tin deposits in Caucasus, in Persia, and very small veins are mentioned for the area of today's Eskehir in Asia Minor. Today, tin is extracted from the metalliferous districts of Malaysia, West Indies, Bolivia, Thailand, China, Japan, Cornwall and Portugal.

I would like to suggest the existence of a relationship between the Greeks and the British based on the following assumptions:

Since the Greeks (before the War of Troy) imported tin from Great Britain with which they produced bronze, as we already mentioned, then the bronze items must have had a portion of tin.

There is no doubt that the bronze items of the Minoic and Mycenaean period have a portion of tin. This was confirmed by analysing bronze items at the chemical laboratory of the Geological

Survey Department of Cyprus by chemist-mining engineer Mr Koumenis. But this does not confirm that tin came from Britain. Thus, I organised a research project for the determination of the trace elements of the cupriferous minerals of Cyprus as well as of the bronze items. Then, we planned the same trace-element research for the tin deposits of Britain and Portugal. The absence of those elements from the minerals of Cyprus and generally of the Greek areas would have provided clues concerning the provenance of tin. We were restricted to the study of those deposits because these are the ones, which are mentioned by the ancient writers. For this, we have asked in writing, via the Consul of Portugal, for the provision of tin samples from Portugal. We received the samples within one month and kindly asked Professor of Geology D. F. Strong from Memorial University of Newfoundland (Canada) to determine the trace elements of our samples. Dr Strong came to Cyprus to study the ultrabasic rocks as part of a separate project. On 5 January 1973, we received from Professor Strong the analyses, which are presented below.

Elements	Sample 1 (ppm)	Sample 2 (ppm)	Sample 3 (ppm)
Zr - Zircon	139	126	153
Sr - Strontium	200	98	496
Rb - Rubidium	46	29	155
Cu - Copper	10	10	10
Ba - Barium	10	10	10
Sn - Tin	25058	241	138103
Mo - Molybdenum	3739	3864	6459
Bi - Bismuth	5826	2506	17669
Bb - Lead	65191	2032	341826

Figure 26 - Analyses of tin minerals from Portugal

The presence of Cobalt and Germanium was not detected, not even in parts per million (ppm).

During the course of the project we were assisted by the work of R. F. Tylecote. In his book Metallurgy in Archaeology (p. 3), he presents the results of his research at the Royal School of Mines (Res. Reports, 1950-53, London 1954, p. 26).

He found traces of Germanium and Cobalt in the tin minerals of Cornwall. Germanium was not found in tin minerals of other known deposits elsewhere. Consequently, the bronze items that were made of tin from Cornwall must contain traces of Germanium.

Since we confirmed that Germanium was absent from the deposits of Portugal then if it were found in the bronze items of Cyprus it would have meant that tin has been imported from Britain. We proceeded with the study of cupriferous minerals of Cyprus for the detection of traces of Germanium. Because this study could not be conducted in Cyprus due to the lack of technical means, we sent some mineral specimens to Britain.

Fig. 27 - Map of Cyprus showing the locations of cupriferous deposits

The results of the analyses were kindly provided to us by Dr G. Constantinou and were part of his Ph.D. thesis titled "Geology and genesis of sulphide deposits of Cyprus".

I cite the results of the analyses of the samples from the four large copper deposits of Cyprus, namely Skouriotissa, Mousoulos Mine (Kalavasos), Mathiatis, and Mitsero (Figure 27).

Originally, it was observed that many samples from different depths of the deposits contain cobalt, nickel, silver, magnesium, chromium, vanadium, titanium, molybdenum, lead, and potassium. Germanium is totally absent. The results are given in ppm.

Elements	**Skouriotissa (ppm)**	**Mousoulos Mine (ppm)**	**Mathiatis Mine (ppm)**	**Mitsero Mine (ppm)**
Co-Cobalt	1079	77	2,5	69
Ni-Nickel	40	17	18	24,7
Ag-Silver	2	1,2	4,2	5,8
Ag-Radioactive Silver	3,7	8,5	1	7
Mn-Manganese	30	3	30	44
Cu-Cuprum	10	7,4	4	14
V-Vanadium	10	17,5	8,5	23
Ti-Titanium	91	42,7	145,7	98
Mo-Radioactive Molybdenum	24	18,8	3	47,8
Pb-Radioactive Lead	9	39,4	10,5	90
Ga-Radioactive Gallium	–	–	–	1

Fig. 28 - Analyses of samples from copper mines of Cyprus.

The analyses were performed by G. Constantinou.

We had no other option but to contact the management of the Cyprus Museum and the National Museum of Greece to obtain fillings from items made out of bronze to be analysed for Germanium.

Elements	**(ppm)**
S - Sulphur	35,9%
Cu - Copper	20,5%
Cd - Cadmium	30
Se - Sellenium	26
Te - Tellurium	14
Ti - Titanium	<5
In - Indium	<5
Ga - Gallium	20
Ge - Germanium	**<5**
Au - Gold	2,3
Ag - Silver	25
Zn - Zinc	1,5%
As - Arsenic	0,15%
C - Carbon	12,5%
Sb - Antimony	0,30%
Ba - Barium	<10

Fig. 29- Analyses of Copper Concentrated Sample of Hellenic Mining Company. The analysis has been performed by Robertson Research Mineral Technology of the United Kingdom.

Before we started this difficult task, we applied to the Hellenic Mining Company Ltd in Cyprus to find out whether they have done any analytical work on their deposits. They informed us that they analysed samples of concentrated copper ore, up to 20%, and they provided us with the results, which are presented below (Figure 28). Because Germanium was present, even in quantities of less than 5 ppm, we were forced to postpone the study of ancient bronze items. Our findings concluded that the presence of Germanium in bronze items could have resulted from the use of Cyprus minerals.

Because it is well known that Cyprus copper has been exported to many places in the world since the antiquity, it is obvious that the same would have happened with the bronze of circum-Mediterranean people. However, the exclusion of Germanium as an element for the proof of the presence of ancient Greeks in Britain strengthens the significance of the other facts on which the present study was based on. These include the references in ancient writings and the various items of Greek origin that have been discovered in Britain.
In this Chapter, we described the presence of large tin deposits in SW Britain (Cornwall). When tin is mixed with copper (1:9 ratio) the alloy bronze is created that has improved properties. The first people to use bronze were in Mesopotamia. The writings of Pliny,

Diodorus of Sicily, and Strabo provide information for the origin, method of extraction and processing, and transport of tin by the Mycenaeans in Greece. Our study on the trace elements deriving from the tin deposits of Europe and the copper deposits of Cyprus casts doubt on the theory proposed by the Royal School of Mines. Specifically, the presence of Germanium in the copper deposits of Cyprus indicates that bronze items that contain this element are not necessarily made of Cornwall-derived tin. We also reported that in Cyprus there is still arsenic-containing copper in small quantities. The presence of ancient Greeks in Britain during the era of metals is due to the taking of tin, which was necessary for the ancient Greeks because they were living in the bronze era.

Written Statements from Ancient Texts Concerning the Presence and Motives of Greeks in Britain

On the same subject, Diodorus from Sicily mentions in his book (Βιβλιοθήκη Ιστορική, 1st Century BC, V22).

Diodorus Siculus, Book V, 22

Those who inhabit Britain towards the cape called Velerion are extremely hospitable and because of their dealings with foreign merchants they have a civilized way of life. They extract the tin, working skilfully the earth that bears it. This earth, being stony, contains veins of earth, and from these they extract the ore, which they clean by melting it. Placing the ore in moulds in the shape of ankle-bones, they carry it to a certain island, which is near Britain and is called Iktis; because at the time of the ebb-tide, the area between this island and Britain is dried up and they carry in carriages large amounts of tin. And something similar happens in the neighbouring islands, which lie between Europe and Britain; because at the time of the flood-tide, when the in-between space is filled, they look like islands, while at the time of the ebb-tide, the sea recedes and dry land is uncovered and they are look like peninsulas. From there (from Iktis) the merchants buy the tin from the natives and carry it to Gaul; and finally, walking through Gaul for up to thirty days, they carry their loads on horseback towards the estuary of the river Rhone.

Figure 30 - Routes and methods for the transfer of tin from Cornwall to Greece.

He also mentions in V38 of the same book the following:

Tin is also extracted in many areas of Iberia, but is not to be found on the surface of the earth, as some relate in their histories, but it is extracted and melted in the same way as silver and gold. Because there are many tin mines beyond Lusitania and on the islands in the ocean near Iberia, which are named Kassiterides because of that reason. Much tin is also carried from the isle of Britain towards Gaul, which lies on the opposite side, and it is carried on horseback by the merchants, through inland Keltike, to the Massaliotai and the city called Narvona; the latter city is a colony of the Romans, and because of its opportune position it enjoys great trade in those lands.

On the same subject, Strabo (1st century BC; CI47.3-2-9) states:

He says that tin is not found on the surface of the earth, as the historians say, but it is extracted; it is found at the barbarians who live beyond the Lusitanians and in the Kattiterides Islands, and from Britain it is transferred to Massalia. But in the land of the Artavroi, who live furthest on the northwest of Lusitania, the earth grows silver, tin and white gold (because it is mixed with silver), and this earth is brought by the rivers; and the women dig it up and wash it through woven filters. This is, then, what he said about the metals.

Then, he writes generally about life in Britain (p. XX):

In parallel with the reports mentioned above, we also have a statement by Pliny (1st century BC, H. N. Book 34, Chapter XXXIV.XLVII - 156, Publisher LOEB; translated from Latin; 23-76 BC).

Pliny, Natural History, Book XXXIV, XLVII

There follows the nature of lead, which is of two types, black and white. The most valuable of the two is the white lead, which the Greeks named cassiteros, and a legend is narrated that they went with ships to the islands of the Atlantic Ocean in order to obtain it and importing it in coated vessels made of osiers and covered with stitche hids. Now it is certain that it is found in Lusitania and Galicia, on the surface level, sandy and of black colour. It can be located by its weight, but also small pieces of this material can be found, mostly in dried up torrents. They wash this sand of the metal and what remains they heat in furnaces. It is also found in the mines of gold which they call 'alutiae', where the flowing water brings out the small pieces of tin, which have small white spots and are of the same weight as gold, so they remain in the baskets in which they collect gold; later they are separated in the furnaces, they are melted and end up as white lead. Black lead is not to be found in Galicia, while in the neighbouring Cantabria black lead abounds; silver cannot be extracted from white lead, while it can be obtained from black lead. Black lead may not be joined to black, without white, neither may it be joined with it without oil, nor may white be joined to itself without black. According to Homer, white lead was important at the time of the Iliad, and he called it cassiterus. Black lead may originate from two sources; it either comes from a vein of its own, mixed with nothing else, or it is created with silver, and the two veins are mixed. From this, the part that becomes liquid first in a furnace is called stagnum; the second is called argentum; what remains in the furnace is called galena, which is the third part of the vein; if it is fused again it gives black lead, minus two parts out of nine.

The next issue are the properties of lead (Pb) which can be either black or white. In Pliny's writings, references to white lead are meant for tin. White lead, or tin, is more precious. The Greeks named it kassiteros (tin) and there was a mythical story about their trips to the Atlantic Ocean where they went to obtain it and bring it back in specially-made baskets, lined with animal hide.

Figure 31 - Image of a clayey plaque discovered in Corinth (from the 6th century BC) showing Greek miners transporting metals in baskets.

In the Penzance Bay in Cornwall, the water level during the change of the tide is marked. During high tide the region of Iktis is converted from a peninsula to an island (Figure 32). During low tide, the region is accessible by land and at this time, ingots of tin are brought by carriages. They are then put on boats during high tide for their transport to Greece. The same natural phenomenon can still be observed. It is known that tin comes from the regions of Lysitania and Kalaikia (Portugal). It can be found on the superficial layers that are sand-like and have black colour. It can be distinguished because of its heavy weight and because small pieces of it can be found on the dried banks of rivers. Especially skilled workers wash the sand that contains tin and, after it is heated in furnaces, collect it as a precipitate.

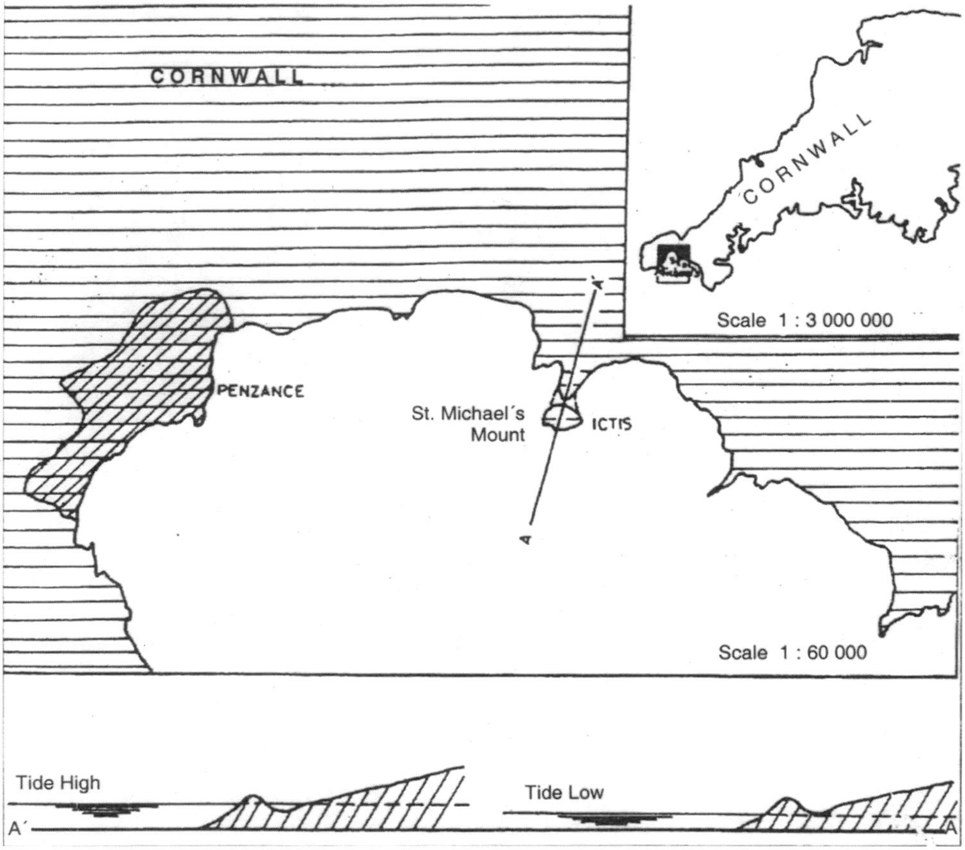

Figure 32 - Map of the Penzance bay of Cornwall.

Homer states that white lead (tin) was heavily used, even during the Trojan War, and he uses the term "Kassiteros".

Based on the items mentioned above, it can be said that the

inhabitants of ancient Greece, prior to 2000 BC, travelled to the British Isles to find and bring metals to Greece. This can be supported by the possible use of tin during the Minoan civilisation of Crete (p.152, 155), or the use of tin by the Mycenaeans. The latter is supported by the discovery of objects in Britain that were obviously influenced by the Mycenaean style. Most likely, Greeks travelled to find and bring back tin and gold. Even though they might have brought other metals, the written record includes only references to the collection, treatment, and transport of tin.

Diodorus from Sicily mentions that the inhabitants of cape Velerio (West Cornwall) had good relations with foreign traders. Tin in this region was collected from ores in granite-rich formations. Then it was melted, in special furnaces, which were found in the region of Chun Castle. Tin was poured into moulds, and transferred to Iktis with carriages during low tide. Tradesmen would buy them and transfer them to Gaul on boats and then on horses for a 30-day trip to the estuary of the river Rhone (modern-day Marseilles). Strabo simply mentions that tin has transferred from the Kattiterides Islands to Marseilles.

In contrast to Diodorus, Strabo describes the collection of tin from sediments and not from ores.

Pliny (p. 102) also mentions the collection of tin from river sediments and its transport to Greece was done in baskets lined with hide.

The use of baskets for the collection and transfer of metals was employed by ancient Greek miners as can be seen on a painting on a pot from the 6th century BC. To find hides for the lining of baskets it is possible that they travelled to Salisbury valley where agriculture was developed.

The mention of the Kattiterides Islands by ancient geographers and historians has been discussed and argued. In my opinion the issue is simple. These islands are Britain, with the tin-rich region of Cornwall and the gold-rich region of Wicklow (Ireland). Both islands and smaller ones like Iktis, are called by the ancient writers as "Ocean's Islands".

What we have mentioned above could be proven by the findings and geography of the region. A plaque made of tin and in the shape of an ankle was discovered in Cornwall, as shown in the picture above. Its length is 2 feet and 10 inches and weighs 258 pounds. It can be found in the Truro Museum of Cornwall. Chronologically, is believed to be before the Roman Period. Its existence supports the statements of Diodorus (p.99).

At the Chun Castle in Cornwall, and at least two other areas, specialised tin-burning furnaces have been discovered (R. E. Tylecote -

Metallurgy in Archaeology, p. 64). They date back to the Roman Period. Thus, we are obliged to accept what has been described above regarding the processing of tin, as a true representation. The description of Diodorus, that tin was transferred to Iktis during low tide, is supported by the topography of the region.

Even the island mentioned by him, Iktis, can be seen today. It is south west of the town of Penzance in Cornwall and today is called both St. Michael Mount and with its ancient Iktis.

These islands can still connect to the main land by a strip of land that appears during low-tide.

Diodorus's reference to the island of Iktis is supported by the topography that exists today.

From my own observations near the coast of South Britain, I discovered that the change in water level between low and high tide can reach 8 metres. In the open sea, at the estuary of the Avon River near Southampton, the change can exceed 5 metres. Two photos, one at low and one at high tide are shown (Figure 33).

Figure 33 - Low and high tide by the river Avon in South Britain.

When Caesar attacked Britain (55 BC), his fleet reached the estuary of the Avon River during high tide. The fluctuation of the water level during the tidal change can reach 5 metres. Because the nearby land is flat, at high tide 3-4 square miles of sea can be seen. At low tide when the water level drops, the flat land dries out and the Avon River appears as a small creek. Caesar's fleet was destroyed during low tide.

CHAPTER 5

GREEK NAMES IN BRITAIN

The presence of the Ancient Greeks in Britain is also testified by the Greek names of cities, rivers, islands, bays, promontories and groups of people, which were in use until the time of the Roman conquest, in the first century AD. These words are presented below, together with the proofs of their Greek origins. On the maps of Britain the positions of these elements are identified, whenever the written sources allow us to do so.

Some authors who have dealt with this topic impress the reader with their attempt to draw Britain away from everything that is Greek. A.L.F. Rivet and Colin Smith, in their book "The Place-Names of Roman Britain" (p.200), claimed that the British list had some connection with a Greek source during its transmission to Ravenna, since "no fewer than 25 names from all parts of the British list still retain a Greek inflexion or case-ending. This illustrates the danger of considering the British section as something apart from the rest of the Cosmography, for vaguely Greek-seeming forms occur sporadically throughout it".

Unfortunately for the supporters of this view, they should know that the Greek names are not only twenty-five, but more than ninety. And together with all the other indications, which testify to the presence of the Ancient Greeks in Britain, this truth is believed beyond any doubt. Certainly more recent British researchers support the view that these names were brought by Greek sea-farers. As if it is possible for some mere passing seafarers to leave their marks in all extent of Britain, and even up to Thoule (Thole), the present-day Iceland. Pytheus was not a seafarer. He was a researcher who desired to learn the unknown. The engraved Mycenaean daggers could not have been engraved by passers-by. Special talent and a lot of time was needed in order for them to be engraved. Also, we should consider the tin trade of Cornwall by the Mycenaeans, the written testimonies of the ancient historians, geographers and philosophers, and many more elements.

In addition to the existing evidence to consider we should add the one mentioned by the Roman author Solinus, in AD 250. In his book *Collectanea Rerum Memorabillium* (22, 1-12) he writes: *"In the vastness an altar inscribed with Greek letters proves that Ulysses was driven to Caledonia"*.

These names are presented below, together with maps showing their possible positions.

NAMES OF ISLANDS

Βρεττανία - Brettania

All ancient historians, geographers and philosophers refer to the island with the name Βρετανική (Bretanike).

Diodorus Siculus (Book XVI, 15) calls the inhabitants of Britain Vrettioi because most of them are slaves; according to the dialect of the natives, fugitives were called *vrettioi.*

Pytheas (AD 320) is the first one to refer to the island with the name *Πριταννική* (Britannike).

Βριτόμαρτις (Britomartis) is a Minoan-Cretan goddess.

Βριτύ = γλυκύ sweet

Μάρτις = παρθένος virgin

Britomartis = sweet virgin.

Bretanos = king of Bretany when Hercules visited his place.

Αλβιών - Albion

Aristotle, the Greek philosopher, refers to the island with the name of *Αλβιών* (Albion).

Strabo calls the Alps (Δ.202) *Αλβία* (Albia).

Αλβιών (Albion) was the son of Neptune, brother of Derkinos, who lived in N. West Italy and was killed by Hercules.

Ορκάδες Νήσοι - Orkades

They are to be found above Scotland.

Όρκη (Orke) = a species of cetacean, relative to the dolphin.

Μυκήναι - Myggenais

It is to be found above Scotland. It is an island of the complex of the Faroe Islands. It is said that the inhabitants of this island have customs similar to those of the ancient Mycenaians.

Άνδρου Έρημος - Adru Erimos

Άντρου = Andros

Έρημος = Desert

It is to be found near the eastern coast of Ireland. Uninhabited island.

Άνδρος (Andros) = An island of the Cyclades in Greece.

Άνδρος (Andros) = Son of Aeneas or of Rhadamanthys. He had the gift of foresight.

Λίμνου Έρημος - Limnou Erimos

Λίμνου = Lemnos

Έρημος = Desert

It is to be found near the eastern coast of Ireland. Uninhabited island.

Thoule - Θούλη

Name of Island

Θολή = blur atmosphere

Θάνατος - Tanatus - Thanet

It is situated on the coast of S.E. Britain. Its soil killed the snakes. Snakes could not live there. Today it is a health resort of Britain.

Μαλέας - Malaia

It is situated in N. W. Scotland

Μαλέας = Peninsula in the Peloponnese.

Μαλαία (Malaia). Ancient city of Arcadia.

Ίκτις - Ictis

A small island in the bay of Penzance of Cornwall.

Ίκτις (Ictis) = a rodent

Aristotle mentions (21.6126) «Η ικτίς εστί μεν το μέγεθος».

Μόνα - Mona

Island of the Western Wales.

Μονάς άδος (Monas) = Unit.

Σκίτις - Scitis

It is situated in N.W. and N. Scotland

Sciton = a species of insects

Σκίτων (Sciton) = An Athenian who was condemned for corruption.

Κοκκίον - Coccium

An island of Scotland.

Κόκκος.

Daruveda

An island of Scotland.

Δρυς (English Deru or Daru) = oak

Δάρυλλος (Daryllos) = name given to the oak by the Ancient Macedonians.

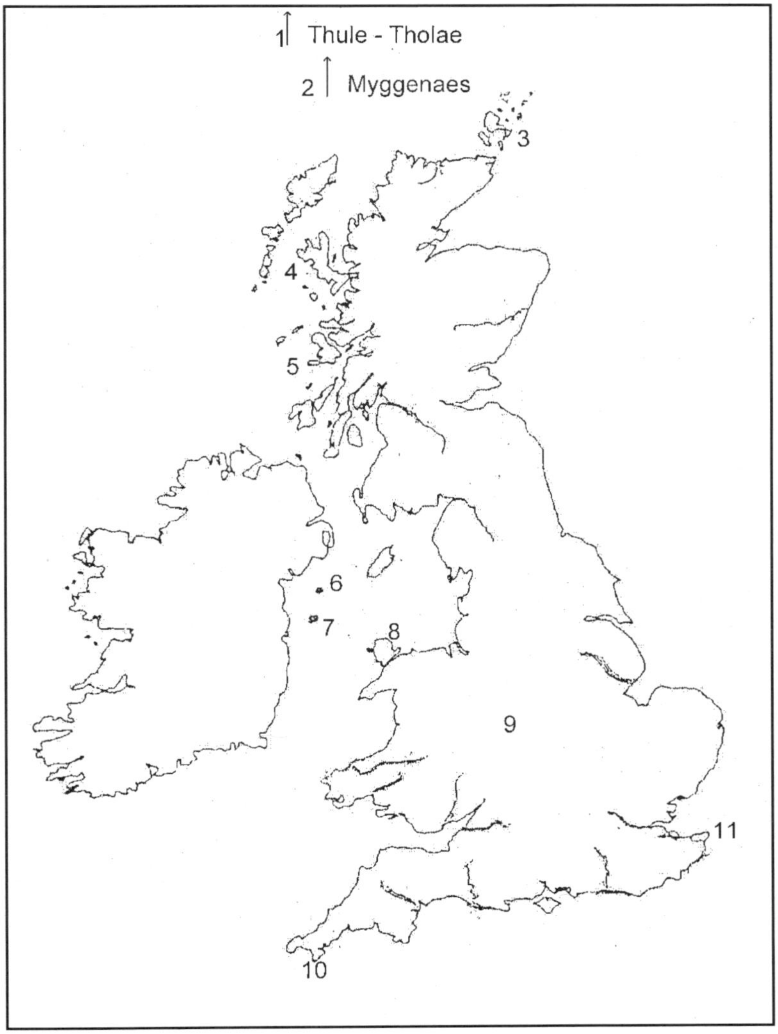

1. Thule - Tholae
2. Myggenaes
3. Orcades
4. Scitis
5. Malaia
6. Adru Erimos
7. Limnu Erimos
8. Mona
9. Albion - Britania
10. Ictis
11. Tanatus
    Coccium
    Daruveda

Figure 34 - Names of islands in Roman Britain

2. NAMES OF CITIES

Ύσκα - Isca

City of S. Britain.

Ύσκα (Yska) = a fungus

Λευκομάγος - Leucomagus

City of S. Britain.

Λευκός Μάγος (Leukos Magos) = White magician

Αντερίδα - Anderitum

Town of S. Britain.

Αντερείδω αντιστηρίζω = support, buttress up

Ανδειράς άδος = ditch-like sewer

Theocritus (s.53). «προς ρόδα των άνδηρα παρ αιμασίαισι πέφυκε».

Καισαρομάγος - Caesaromagus

City of S.E. Britain.

Καίσαρ (Kaisar) = Caesar

Μάγος (Magos) = Wizard

Οθόνη-αι - Othona-ae

City of S. E. Britain.

Οθωνοί (Othonoi) = Islands of the Ionian Sea in Greece.

Οθόνη (Othone) = screen, sheet, canvas

Κορίνιον - Corinium

City of S. Britain.

Κορίνεον (Corineon) = ancient city of Cyprus

Κόριννα (Corinna) = species of spidery

Κόριννος (Corinnes) = species of birds

Λιμάνι - Portus

City of S. Britain.

Λιμάνι (Limani) = Port

Alauna

City of Central and N. Britain.

Αλαίος Απόλλων - Αλύσιον πεδίον

Αλαός (Alaos) = blind, species of beetle

Alaunocelum

Άλη (Ale) = error, fallacy

Οκέλλω (Okello) = fall to the shore

Λίνδος - Lindum

City of Central Britain.

Λίνδος (Lindos) = a city of the island of Rhodes in Greece

Λίνδος (Lindos) = a river in Asia Minor

Λίνδος (Lindos) = name of an aromatic plant

Λίνδος (Lindos) = species of insects

Εμποράκιον - Eburacum

City of Central Britain.

Εμπόριον (Emporion) = Commerce

Καταρράκτης - Cataractonium

City of Central Britain.

Καταρράκτης (Katarraktes) = catarract

Υδατοφράκτης (Hydatophraktes) = dam

Strabo (14.01.21) writes «Τηρήσας καταρρακτήν όμβρον συνήργησε».

Καταρράκτης (Catarractes) = a species of birds.

Leucovia

City of N. Britain. *Λευκόν (Leuco)* = white

Trimontium

City of N. Britain.

Tri Τρία (Tria) = three

Κόρια - Coria

City of N. Britain.

Κόρια (Koria) = a name used for the goddesses Artemis and Athena.

Κούριον (Curium) = city of Kourios Apollo in Cyprus

Κουρείο (Koureio) = a sacred place

Κούρος (Kouros) = a young man

Πτερωτόν Στρατόπεδον - Pteroton Stratopedon

Winged Camp – City of Scotland

Μεγαρίς - Megaris

City of Britain.

Μεγαρίς (Megaris) = an ancient name of the city of Megara in Greece.

Μεγαρίς (Megaris) = a city of the Megaris in Sicily.

Καινός Λιμήν - New Harbor (Port) - Kenos Limin

City of S. Britain.

Όχθη Υψηλή - Ochthi Ipsili

City of Scotland.

Μέγας Λιμήν - Megas Limin

City of S. Britain.

Χορδή - Corda Κόρτα

City of Central Britain.

Ύστατα Θερμά - Istata Therma

City of S. Britain.

Δευτέρα Σεβαστή - Deftera Sebasti

City of S. Britain.

Octapita

Οκτώ - eight

Ταμείον - Tameia

City of Wales.

Ταμείον (Tameion) = Treasury

Νοιομάγος - Neomagus - New magician

City of S. Britain.

Λεγιών Κ. - Legion K.

City of Central and South Britain.

Νικηφόρος - Nikiforos

City of Central Britain.

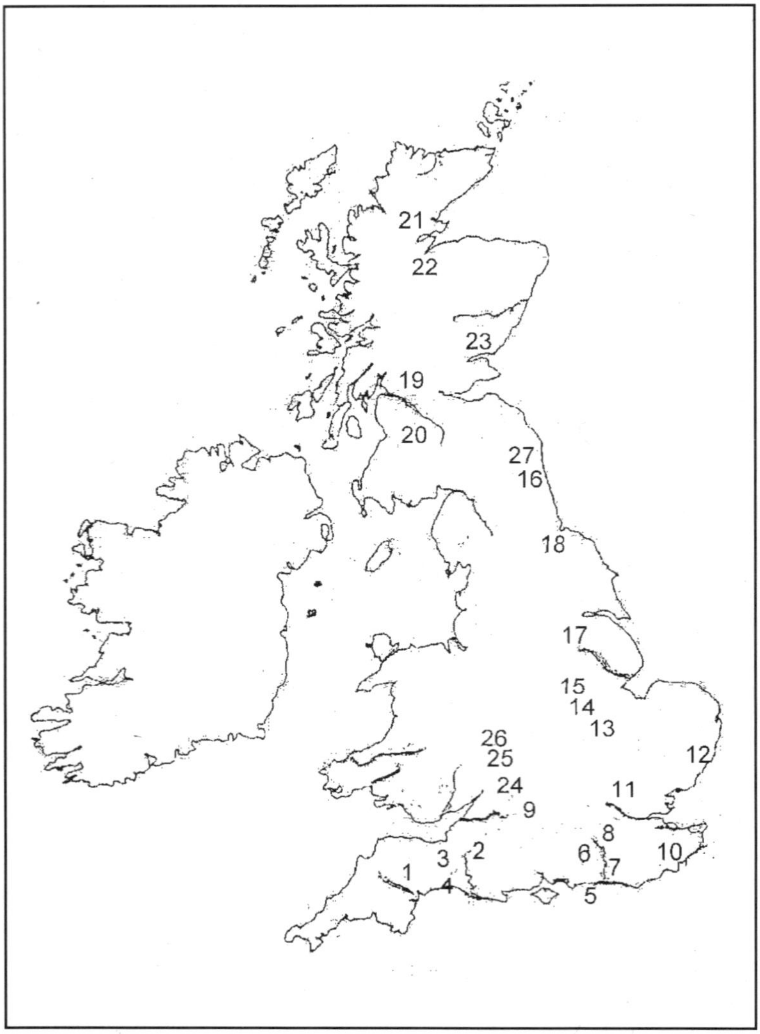

1. Isca
2. Istata Therma
3. Legion
4. Deftera Sebasti
5. Megas Limin
6. Kaenos Limin
7. Trisantonus
8. Neomagus
9. Leucomagus
10. Anderitum
11. Caesaromagus
12. Othona-ae
13. Lindum
14. Nikiforos
15. Legion K.
16. Alauna
17. Eburacum
18. Cataractonium
19. Coria
20. Leucovia
21. Tamia
22. Ochthi Ipsili
23. Pteroton Stratopedon
24. Corinium
25. Alaunocelum
26. Tripontium
27. Megaris
    Linani
    Corda
    Octapita

Figure 35 - Names of cities in Roman Britain

3. NAMES OF RIVERS

Isca - Ύσκα

River in S. Britain.

Ύσκα (isca) = name of funghi

Leuca - Λευκά - White

River of Wales

Trisantona - Τρεις - Three

River of E. and N. Britain.

Τρεις (treis) = Three

Clota - Γλώττα - σσα - tongue

River of W. Scotland

Axium - Αξιός

River of N. Britain.

Άξιος (Axios) = competent

Stuctia - Στακτύς

River of Wales.

Στακτύς = grey, ash-coloured

Longus - Λόγγος

River of W. Scotland.

Λόγγος (Longos) = thick forest

Loxa - Λοξός

River of E. Scotland.

Vedra - Ύδρα - Ύδωρ - Water

River of E. Britain.

Eitis - Ίτυς

Ίτυς (Itys) = name of an ancient Greek hero.

Ίτυς (Itys) = circumference of a wheel.

Iliad of Homer: «οφρα ίτυν κάμψη»

Xen. (An. 4.7.12): «ίτυς βλεφάρων» = arched curve of the brow

Clyde - Κλύδων - Κλύδιον

River of N.W. Britain.

Κλύδων (Klydon) = tempest

Κλύδιον (Klydion) = the open sea

Argidas - Άργος

Άργος ους (Argos) = white

Αργός = idle, unemployed

Logias

Λέγω (Lego) = choose - speak

Vetra - Ύδρα - Ούεδρα ποταμού - estuary of river

Tanaus - Δαναός

Estuary of river in N. Britain.

Mentioned in Agricola On Britain.

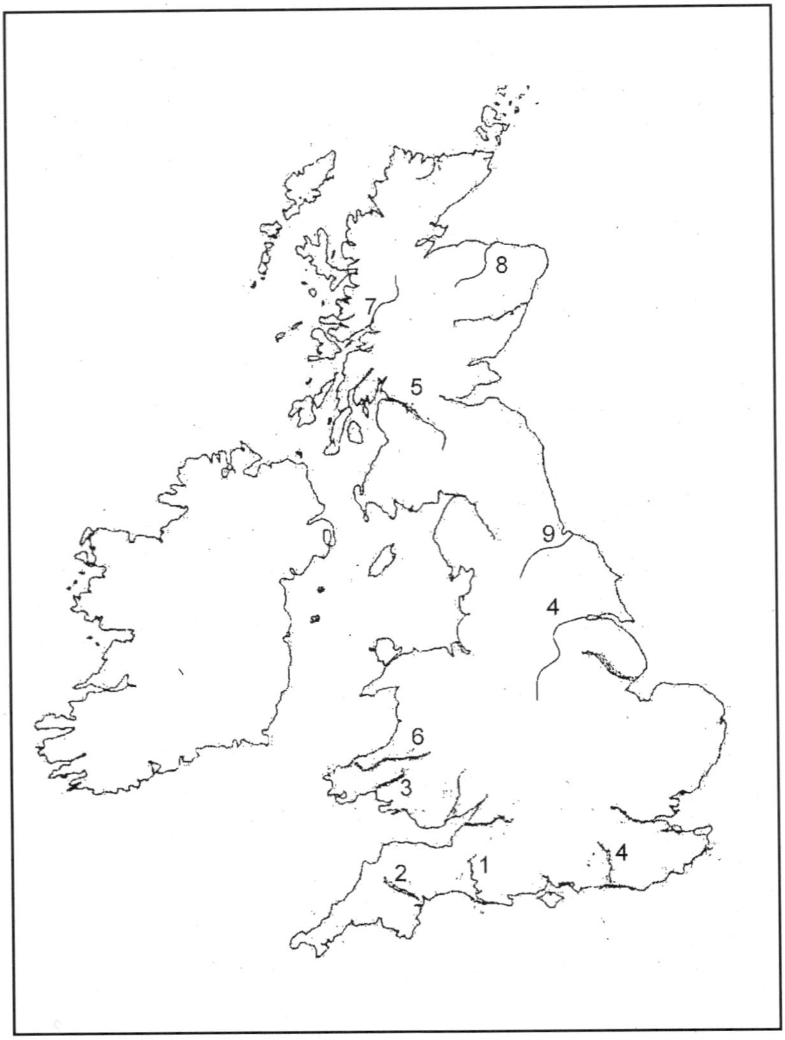

1. Isca
2. Tamara
3. Leuca
4. Trisantoni
5. Glota
6. Stuctia
7. Longus
8. Loxa
9. Vedra

Axium
Eidis
Clyde
Argidas
Logias
Vedra
Toesibis
Tanaus

Figure 36 - Names of rivers in Roman Britain

4. NAMES OF PROMONTORIES AND BAYS

Ηρακλέους Άκρον - Hercules Promontory

Promontory in the S. W. Britiain

Ορκάς Άκρον - Orcas Promontory

Promontory in Scotland

Ορκάς (Orkas) = species of cetaceans

Όκελον Ακρωτήριον - Ocelum Promontory

Promontory of E. Britain

Οκέλλω (Okello) = fall to the shore

κέλλω

Homers Odyssey: «νήα κέλσαι» = drive a ship to the shore

Antivestaeum Promontory

Promontory of S. W. Britain

Αντί Εστία (Hestia) = Goddess Hestiades

Latin Vestaeum

Pytheas named it Velerion.

Οκταπίταρον Άκρον - Octapitarum Promontory

Promontory in W. Britain

Οκτώ (Okto) = eight

Βόρειον Άκρον - North Promontory

Αλίμενος Κόλπος - Alimenos Bay

Bay in E. Britain.

Αλίμενος Κόλπος = Bay without port

Κάντιον Άκρον - Cantion Promontory

Promontory in S. W. Britain.

Ευλίμενος Κόλπος - Eulimenos Bay

Bay of W. Britain

ευ (eu) = good

λιμήν (limen) = harbour

Εξοχή - Exoche

Promontory of W. Britain

Εξοχή = countryside

Φωταπίταρον Άκρον - Photapitaron Promontory

φως φωτός (phos) = light

επίδαυρος (epidauros) = dense, bright

Ανινόου - Χερσόνησος Άκρον

Αλκί-νοος a Greek name

Λιμαννόνιος Κόλπος - Lemannonius Bay

Bay of W. Scotland.

Μεταρίς Ίσχυσις - Metaris

Bay of E. Britain.

Μετάρροια (Metarroia) = low water, flow to the opposite direction, form a tide

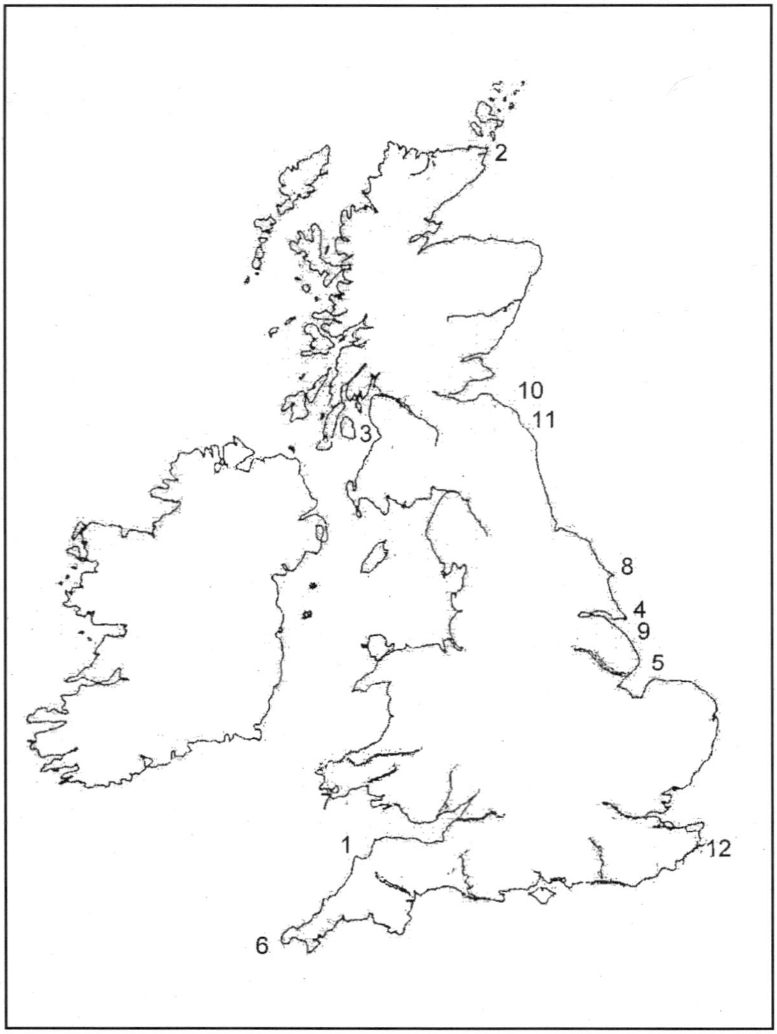

1. Hercules prom.
2. Orcas prom.
3. Lemannonius bay
4. Ocelum prom.
5. Eulimenos bay
6. Antivestaeum prom.
7. Octapitarum prom.
8. Exoche
9. Metaris
10. Boteria
11. Alimenos Bay
12. Kantion prom.
    Photapitaron prom.
    Aninoos prom.

Figure 37 - Names of promontories and bays

5. NAMES OF PLACES AND GROUPS OF PEOPLE

The location of some of these in Britain is unspecified

Cornwall - Κορνουάλη

Region of S. W. Britain.

Κόρνου και άλη

Κέρας, κόρνος = horn

αλς ός = sea

Κόρνου άλη

Abissum - Άβυσσος

Region of Central Britain.

Άβυσσος = abyss, great depth of the sea, the Hades.

Argistillum - Αργήστυλλον

Region of Britain.

Αργώ και Στύλλος.

Αργώ Αργοναύται

Άργος = City of Greece.

Στήλη (stele) = column

Caesaromagus - Μάγος, μαγεία

Military position of the Romans in S.E. Britain

Magus = magician

Canonium - Κανονικός

Military position of the Romans.

Epiacum

Roman fort in Britain.

Έπω = look after

Επειός = son of Panopeus, creator of the Trojan Horse.

Eposessa - Ιππόεσσα

A region with horses in Britain.

Ίππος = horse

Magalonium

Region of Britain.

Μεγαλώνω = grow up

Μεγάλος = big

Pilais - Πύλαι

Region of S. W. Britain.

Πύλη = entrance, gate

Πυλαίος = in front of the gate

Calidonia - Καληδωνία

Name of Scotland

Picti

People of Scotland.

Πήγνυμι, πηκτός = thick

Πηκτίς ίδος = a musical instrument

Anicetis - Ανίκητοι

A group of people of S. Britain.

Decantae - Δεκάδες

Name of a group of people in the area of Flintshire.

Δεκάς = group of ten.

Ancalites - Αγκαλίδες

Name of a group of people of S. E. Britain.

Αγκαλίς ίδος - embrace

Ordovices

Name of a group of people of S. Wales.

Ορδή = undisciplined group of people

Οίκος Οικία = house

Latin vicus = village

Caereni - Κέρωνες

People of N. Scotland.

Καίριος = timely

Κερύνεια = a city of Cyprus and the Peloponnese.

Κέρας, κόρνου = horn

Κρέωνες - Creones

A group of people of Britain.

Κρέων ονος = king

Κορνάβιοι - Cornavi

Inhabitants of the edges.

Κόρνον = horn

Δαμνιόνιοι - Damnioni

A group of people of S. Britain.

δάμνημι = to tame

Σιλύρες - Silyres

A group of people in Wales.

Silyres = dressed in rags

Παρίσοι - Parisi

A group of people in Central Britain.

παρά ίσος = equal distances

Taphouse - On Exmoor

Τάφος - grave

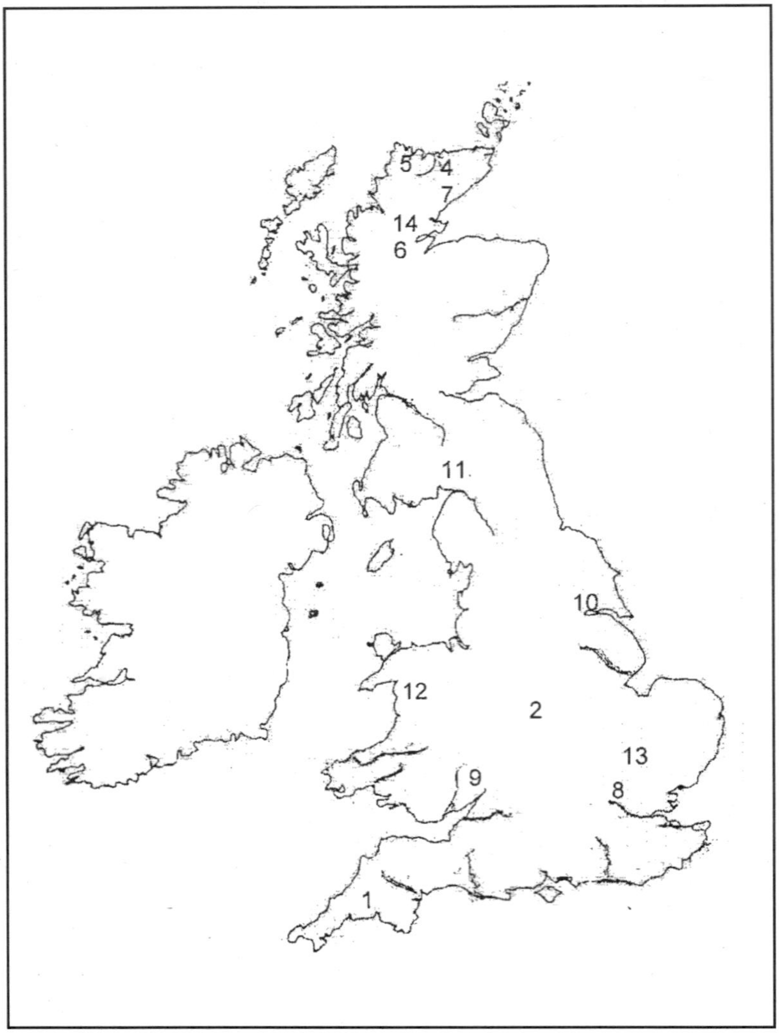

1. Cornwall
2. Abissum
3. Argistillum
4. Caereni
5. Creones
6. Galidonia
7. Decantae
8. Caesaromagus
9. Silyres
10. Parisi
11. Damnoni
12. Ordovices
13. Angalites
14. Picti

Anicetis
Canonium
Epiacum
Eposessa
Pilais
Megalonium
Creones
Cornavi

Figure 38 - Places and Groups of people

CHAPTER 6

HERCULES

Much has been written about the expeditions to Europe, Africa and Asia of the Semi-god Hercules or Herculeses (since we believe that they were more than one).

Hercules was the son of Alcmenes and Zeus. He was born in Thebes, Greece. His name at first was Alkides but Pythia renamed him Hercules to flatter Hera (Zeus wife) who was pursuing him because he was the son of Zeus from another woman.

Hercules lived before Homer's time. His expeditions started from the third millennium A.D. One of his expeditions took place during the Stone age where he made use of his wooden club, and another in the bronze age where he used his bow and arrows and his double axe (which was his symbol).

From all the twelve labors of Hercules, we will talk about the tenth, the stealing of Geryones' herd from an island called by the Greeks

Erytheia. This island lied outside the Herculean Columns on Gadez side. Geriones (name derived from the Greek verb Gerio= to shout) was the son of Chrysaourus and Kalleroe the daughter of Ocean God. He lived on the island of Erytheia. On that island, his herd of cattle was grazing guarded by Evritionas, son of Mars and a monster -dog called Orthos.

Chrysaourus was a very rich and powerful person. He had three sons and a strong army, so Hercules was quite prepared, with expeditionary army and started his assault from the mighty island of Crete*.

References

Apollodorus (Book II, V.10), Herodotus (Book IV 8) and Diodorus of Sicily (Book V. 20. 1-3).

Apollodorus. The Library, II, v.10

As a tenth labour, he was ordered to bring the oxen of Geryones from Erytheia. Erytheia, which is now called Gadeira, was an island lying near the Ocean. In that island lived Gyreones, son of Chrysaor and Kallirroe, daughter of the Ocean. He had the body of three men grown together, joined in one at the belly, but divided into three from the flanks and the thighs. And he had red oxen, the shepherd of which was Eurytion, and their watchdog was Orthos, a two-headed dog born by

* *Prehistoric Crete*, R.W. Hutchinson. p.141

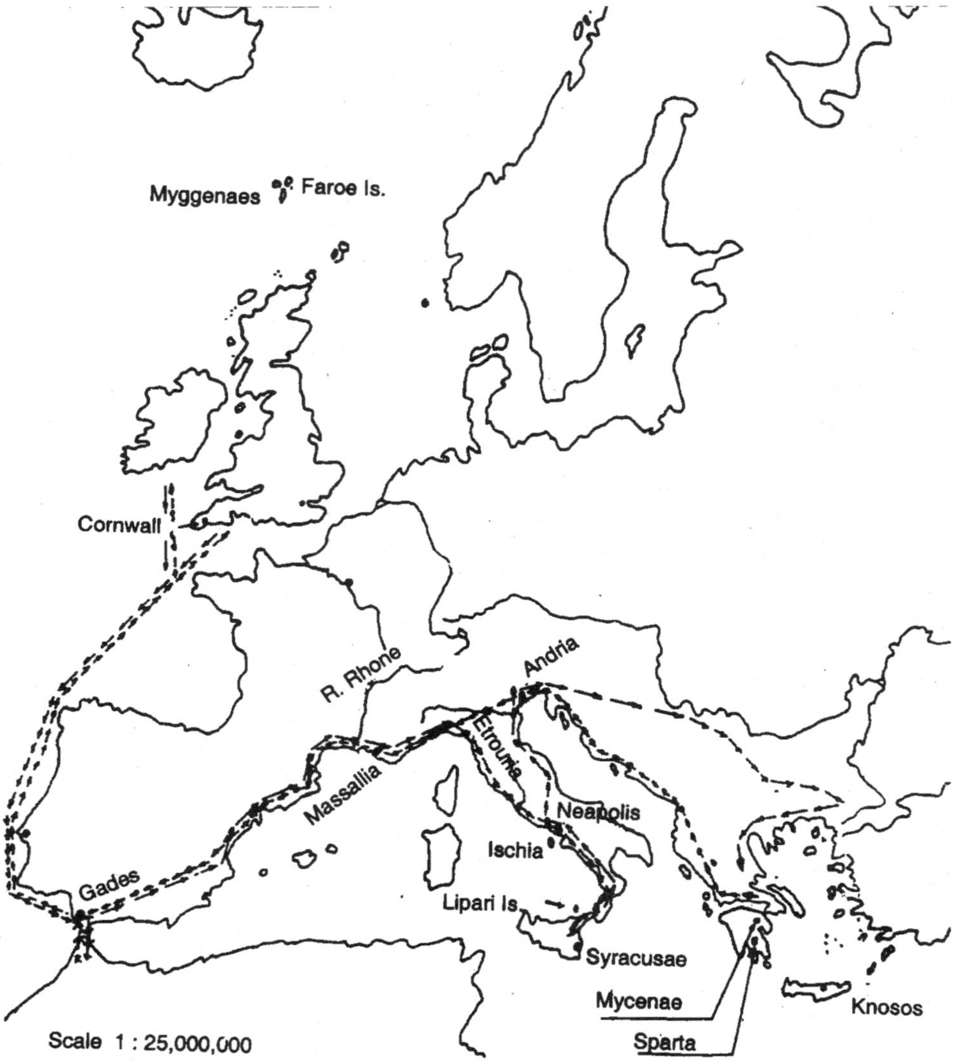

Figure 39 - The course followed by Hercules

Echidna and Typhon. Travelling, then, through Europe towards the oxen of Geryones, he killed many wild beasts and reached Libya, and reaching Tartesson he erected, as landmarks of his journey, two pillars, opposite each other, on the boundaries of Europe and Asia. But, being heated by the Sun on the way, he aimed his bow at the God who, admiring his valour, gave him a golden cup, in which he crossed the Ocean. And reaching Erytheia, he hid in mount Abas. The dog, however, sensing his presence, pounced upon him, but Hercules stroke him with his club, as he did with Eurytion, whom he killed when he tried to help the dog. But Menoites, who was tending the sheep of Hades there, notified Geryones about the event, and the latter, finding Hercules as he was driving the oxen by the river Anthemous, fought against him and died, shot by his bow. And Hercules, placing the oxen in the cup, sailed across to Tartessos and returned the cup to the Sun.

Herodotus. Book IV. 8

This is, then, what the Scythians relate about the land beyond their own, while the Greeks who inhabit the Pontus relate the following: Hercules, driving the oxen of Geryones, reached this land, which was deserted, but is now used by the Scythians. Geryones lived beyond the Pontus, inhabiting the island called by the Greeks Erytheia, on the Ocean beyond the Pillars of Hercules, near Gadeira. As regards the Ocean, they say that it starts from the rising of the sun, flowing through the whole earth, but they do not prove this in practice. From there Hercules arrived to the land now called Scythia, and because there he met winter and cold weather, he put on his lion's skin and fell asleep; at that time, the oxen which were grazing under the yoke, disappeared.

Diodorus of Sicily, Book V. 20. 1-3

The Phoenicians, who continuously sailed from ancient times for trading purposes have established many colonies in Libya, and also not a few of them in the western parts of Europe. And as their ventures proceeded according to schedule, they accumulated great wealth, and attempted to sail beyond the Pillars of Hercules, in the sea which they call Ocean. At first, on the strait of the Pillars itself, on the European side, they built a city, which, being on a promontory, they named Gadeira, in which they erected buildings suitable to the place, and a luxurious temple of Hercules, and they performed magnificent sacrifices, according to the customs of the Phoenicians. And it so happened that this temple was held in high honour both then, and in the more recent times, even to our own days.

From the above references, about the tenth labor, we can assume that:

1. It was not a one person expedition, many took part. This could be assumed by Apollodorus' information that Hercules needed a ship to cross the Ocean and after loading a great number of cattle, he returned to Greece On his journey back ,he had to fight against a lot of different tribes that were living on the Italian Peninsula. He fought and won, and succeeded in bringing the cattle to Thrace and then delivered them to all Greece. Is it possible for this to be the task of only one man, even if that man is Hercules? One man couldn't drive a ship big enough to carry a herd of cattle, travel for several days and nights through the Ocean and arrive at that remote island, fight, catch and load a big herd of cattle and travel across the Ocean to the coasts of Europe and then, by land, lead the herd through Italy, to South Greece. This cannot be only one man's task but that of many. The whole operation must have been a real expedition and must have lasted for a long time.

2. From Herodotus' and Apollodorus' narrations, we can conclude that these "Herculean" campaigns were led by at least two different "Hercules". This is obvious because of the different routes they had followed on the way back. It is also obvious, because of the different means of transport used by "Herculeses" during their trip. At first, both, Herodotus and Apolodorus, referred to the island of Erytheia, as the Ocean island, where both have mentioned the stealing of the herd of Geryones. Herodotus said that Hercules was using a chariot driven by horses, he spent winter in Scythia, lived there with tribes

who were there, had procreated there and affected life and traditions. This is shown by the custom of Scythes to wear the "gold bottle" on their belt, something that they learned from Hercules.
On the other hand, Apollodorus said that Hercules had returned through the Italian peninsula, the coast of Andria and finally to Greece through the Thrace mountains.
Nevertheless, this route was not as idyllic as the other one, because there were fights mentioned, lots of risks, dangers and difficulties. The fact that there is no chariot mentioned, supported the idea that we are talking about two different expeditions.

3. Both Apollodorus and Herodotus mentioned gold. Apollodorus said that Hercules quarreled with the God Helios (the Sun) and the God, appreciating his courage had donated him a gold ship (vessel), which helped him cross the Ocean. Furthermore, Herodotus said that the Scythes, maintained the custom of carrying a "gold bottle" on their belt A custom given to them by Hercules. In our case the precious metal is offered to the man from a God; this might show the Greeks' endeavor, at that time, to find gold in these areas and carry it back to Greece. If this is true, then gold deposits must be found, apart from Britain and Ireland, on the islands of the Ocean, well known by the Greeks.

4. Both writers mentioned that Hercules arrived at the mythical country of Erythea, which was an island outside in the sea, near Gadez, according to Herodotus. According to Apollodorus this island was Gadez. Our point of view is different and is supported by the following arguments: a) Erytheia is an island in the Ocean, either identified with Gadez or not. b) Hercules needed a ship or ships to reach Erytheia and carry a herd of cattle. These ships were given to him by God Helios(the Sun). It also shows that the island was in some distance from the European coasts. c) There was a mountain on the island called Avas. On this mountain herds of cattle were grazing guarded by shepherds and dogs. This doesn't help to identify Erytheia as the island of Gadez. We think that Erytheia is a place in British Island. It is known that Gadez was built by Hercules. Later it was inhabited by the Phoenicians, who had turned it into a fortified position. There was also a luxurious temple, devoted to Hercules, ruins of which can still be found on a small island called Petri, which is what remains of old island of Gadez, that was 25 kilometers long.

The Phoenicians used the island of Gadez as a starting point. They were excellent merchants. They attacked the rich in mines areas of the Pyrenees, Britain and possibly Cornwall. This is written by Diodorus from Sicily, Volume V 35.

Visit of Hercules in the land of Bretanos

Hercules, traveling to Erythea, was hosted by King Bretanos, who was reigning in an area of Britany. The daughter of King Bretanos called Celtini or Celtus, fell in love with Hercules and they had a son called Celtos, the forefather of the Celtoi. The inhabitants of Britany took the name of their nation after Celtos. The Celtoi worshipped Hercules as their God. So at least half of the people of Celtoi were of Greek origin.*

*A. Treror Hodge, Ancient Greek in France, London 1998.

CHAPTER 7

STATEMENTS OF BRITISH ARCHAEOLOGISTS - HISTORIANS- GEOGRAPHERS

1. A TRAVELLERS HISTORY OF GREECE

BY A.R. BURN 1965

P. 14. Western metal was no doubt still a magnet, though the early Cycladic outposts in Spain had been taken over by natives - the "Beaker folk", whose subsequent migrations northaward carried some faint radiation from near eastern culture even to the British Isles. But the closest contacts, especially after about 1600, were with the Greek mainland.

P. 15 Through Greece, influences from the near east reached bronze age Europe. On Salisbury Plain, a chief's grave contained an inlaid scepter "paralleled only", says Professor Piggott, in one of the early shaft-graves of Mycenae. "In Britain too", he adds, "the final monument of Stonehenge, with its architectural competence and sophistication, is best explained in terms of the momentary introduction of superior skills from an area of higher cultlure, which in the circumstances can hardly be other than Mycenae". It is only a few years since there were recognized, cut in one of the stones of that monument, the shapes, shallow, and worn, so that they only strike the eye at a certain angle and in a certain light, of an axe and a dagger of characteristically Mycenaean pattern.

P. 56. A daughter of King Agamemnon of Kyme married Midas, King of Phrygia and a sea - captain named Midakritos ("approved of Midas" - probably a man of Kyme, named for his father's patron) is named as the first man to bring tin from a "Tin Island" in the west. An ancient throne at Delphoi was said to have been a gift of Midas. Eastward, a Midas (it was the name of several Kings) fought the Assyrians in the Taurus mountains; and Phrygia probably supplied tin to the Kingdom of Urartu (Ararat), which also fought the Assyrians at the height of their power, and was famous for its bronze and iron work.

It looks as if in this enterprise the Greeks were deliberately setting out to compete with the Phoenicians, who had their own trade route to the west along the coast of Africa. They had small "factories" at Cadiz (Gaddir in Phoenician, meaning walled place) and on the way to it, ...

2. THE BRITISH ISLES

Homer L. Thomas 1967.

P. 135. Gold cups, some daggers, and double axes suggest a chronological equation with the Shaft Grave period at Mycenae.

3. STONEHENGE AND AVEBURY.

Text bt R.J.C. Atkinson, Professor of Archaeology, University College, Cardiff. London, Her Majestys Stationary Office, 1959.

("The squaring and dressing of the stones, their joints, and the elaborate shaping of the lintels, as well as the high degree of accuracy achieved in placing the stones, all point to influence from the urban civilization of Minoan Crete and Mycenean Greece, in which alone at this time was any sophisticated architecture to be found).

Connections between Britain and the Mediterranean at this period had already been suspected, from the finding in British barrow-burials, some of them close to Stonehenge, of objects imported or copied from Mediterranean sources. In 1953 these connections were dramatically confirmed by the discovery at Stonehenge of carvings of bronze axeheads and a bronze dagger. The axes are all of a type which was made in Ireland and exported to the Continent between 1600 and 1400 B.C.; (but the best match for the dagger comes from the Shaft Graves of Mycenae in southern Greece, the legendary home of Agamemnon).

From this and other evidence the erection of the sarsen stones at Stonehenge can be dated soon after 1500 B.C. The architect (for surely the designer of such a building deserved the title) must almost certainly have been a man who was familiar with the buildings of the contemporary urban civilizations of the Mediterranean world".

4. STUDIES IN MEDITERRANEAN ARCHAEOLOGY, *VO. XVII, I. TEXT. "NEAR EASTERN, MEDITERRANEAN AND EUROPEAN CHRONOLOGY".*

The Historica 1, Archaeological, Radiocarbon, Pollen - Analytical an Geochronological Evidence, 1967 BY HOMER L. THOMAS, Professor of History and Archaeology of the University of Missouri.

IBERIA:

P. 97. Bronze Age. Sometime during the early second millennium, the EL Argaric culture arose in southeastern Spain, ushering in the Spanish Bronze Age. Its cemeteries of cist graves have assemblages showing few foreign contacts. There are horns of consecration similar to those found in the Aegean, but these have little precise chronological value. Faience beads, however, clearly demonstrate that the EL Argaric culture was current in the middle of the second millennium, and had contact with the eastern Mediterranean of Mycenaean times. Chalices are similar to Aegean Kylikes and must be connected with those of the Mycenaean period, suggesting that the formation of this culture should not go back much before the middle of the second millennium.

5. R.W. Hutchinson, PREHISTORIC CRETE, 1965

MINOAN AND MYCENAEAN TRADE WITH THE WEST

P. 113. It is possible of course that some of this western trade may have been carried on not by Minoan Cretans but by Cycladic traders from Phylakopi on Melos.

Isolated vases of a kind made in Melos in the Middle Cycladic period have been found (without context) as far west as Marseille and the Balearic isles, and a stone axe of what seems to be probably Naxian emery at Calne in Wiltshire. The faience beads, however, of Levantine manufacture scattered over Europe, especially Britain, and dated by Piggot between 1550 and 1100 B.C. must be evidence of Mycenaean, not Minoan, trade with the West.

P. 141. During the Second Early Minoan Period 2800 - 2400 B.C. by Evans, 2300 - 2100 by Hutchinson, the eastern people and the Mesara developed their Copper Age Culture to a new height, though the north and west lagged behind them.

Metal tools and weapons are relatively scarce but always of copper or with a very low proportion of tin, to which the Cretans probably had no direct access.

6. SOUTH WEST ENGLAND, by Aillen Fox.

Editor Thames & Hundson 1964

RILLATON CUP

P. 70. The fine gold cup, 3 1/4 inches high, is unique: the horizontal ribbing, and the ribbon-like handle, margined with chased lines and secured by three rivets and diamond-shaped washers, are features that link it with products of Aegean metalworkers. It resembles a pair of small ribbed gold cups from shaft-grave IV, one of the royal tombs in the grave circle at Mycenae, dating from the sixteenth century B.C. The profile at first glance is reminiscent of a Bell-Beaker but in reality it is a softened version of a biconical form which we shall meet again in shale at Farway, or in the gold cup from Fritzdorf, Bonn, which in turn was inspired by Mycenaen shaft-grave models. The Rillaton cup was probably a heirloom when it was placed in the grave with the ogival dagger, and the glass or faience beads in the late fifteenth century B.C.

P. 74. A cemetery of ten barrows near Pelynt, south Cornwall also belongs to this early Bronze Age phase; the barrows, which were excavated in 1830-1845, contained cremations, one with an ogival dagger, another with a greenstone macehead, and with a third was the famous short sword or dagger of late Mycenean type. As professor Gordon Childe pointed out in 1951, this square-shouldered weapon with a flanged hilt plate must have been made in the Aegean, perhaps as early as the fourteenth or thirteenth century B.C., though the closest analogies are the short swords from a tomb at Diakata, Kephallenia, which have been dated to the twelfth century. The pelynt find is of great importance, because it substantiates the recognition of another Mycenaean dagger - an earlier type resembling those in the sixteenth century shaft-grave VI ate Mycenae - which is carved on one of the Sarsen Uprights at Stonehenge.

P. 83. Sporadic Mediterranean imports occur on the south coast at a later date. As well as the sub-Mycenaean dagger from Pelynt there is a double-axe of 94% copper from Mount Howe, Topsham, on the Exe estuary; This with its characteristic oval shaft-hole was undoubtedly made in the Aegean: its closest analogies are in hoards on the Acropolis at Athens and in the late Poros wall area at Mycenae both dating C. 1250 B.C.

7. The Growth of Civilization G. L. Field

ST. MARTIN'S PRESS New York 1966

Mycenaeans in Britain

P. 66. It is just possible that Mycenaeans sailed to Britain, for the outline of a Mycenaean dagger was cut into one of the great upright stones at Stonehenge. Perhaps a clever architect went to show the uncivilized Bronze Age tribes how to build this great open-air temple. Stonehenge was built about 1500 B.C.

P. 67. The Mycenaeans may have gone to Britain for tin, or for slaves and furs, which were also brought overland from Central Europe. The smooth orange fossil resin, amber, was admired by all ancient peoples, and the Mycenaeans obtained it from traders who brought it from the shores of the Baltic Sea.

8. THE GREEKS in the west, A.G. Woodhead, 1962

The ubiquitous faience beads which in a chain of distribution across Europe link Egypt and Britain in continuous evidence of Bronze Age trade, are attested also in the Lipari islands. The British end of this trade connection in strikingly evidenced by the Mycenaean dagger found at Pelynt in Cornwall. Supporting as it does the evidence of the dagger carved on one of the great standing stones of Stonehenge. The Mycenaean material from the Lilpari islands is indeed such that a fullscale settlement, as in the case of Taranto, has suggested for them. A colony has also been proposed for Palermo, though on the more slender basis of the Mycenaean figurines found there.

It may be worth adding that while the principal western relationships are with the Mycenaean culture, there are also traits of contact with Minoan Crete, and these also have left their mark on tradition. But in the past, perhaps under the influence of the tradition, they have been over-estimated, and effectively they amount to little more than a handful of Late Minoan I sherds from Lipari. From this meager evidence there can be no arguments as to direct trade with Crete, and other alleged examples of Cretan influence have been better explained on a Mycenaean basis.

9. Ancient Europe - By Stuart Piggot

Edinburg University press 1965

P. 134 ... The earliest datable contact is in Wessex, where in Bush Barrow on Salisbury Plain a warrior-chieftain was buried with a sceptrer or wand of office in laid with zigzag bone mounts exactly duplicated in Grave iota of the “B” shaft-Graves, with late Middle Helladic pottery, and so a date near 1600 B.C.

Mycenaean metal-working techniques were however now influencing craftsmen in the far north-west; the gold cups from Fritzdorf, near Bonn and Rillaton in Cornwall are instances of this, the latter with corrugated sides as in a pair from the shaft-Graves, and other gold-work from the barrow-burials of the Wessex Culture show similar contacts.

P. 136. These are isolated examples of contact, but more significant are two groups of finds which occur in some numbers; objects decorated with specifically Mycenaean motifs and beads and ornaments of faience, the artificial substance with glass beads much used in the ancient orient and the Aegean.

STONE CIRCLES Rob Roy USA 1999 P. 10

Related to the Heel Stone of Stonehenge Rob Roy says:

"Some writers have surmised that Heel Stone should be spelled Hele Stone, a link to Helios, the Greek sun god.

EPILOGUE

The Greek nation offered Europe its name (Europa was in the Greek mythology the daughter of Aginoras and Tilephassis with whom Zeus, the king of the Gods, fell in love and subsequently abducted her) and for many centuries offered to the people of Europe the religion, the culture and its spirit of civilization.

The European civilization is a synthesis of the Greek, the Roman and the Christian spirit. One synthesis in which the Greek spirit offered the ideas of freedom, scientific and cultural progress, democracy and beauty.

The Roman spirit offered the idea of a well structured and administered empire as well as that of eunomia while Christianity offered tolerance, forgiveness and love.

Some researchers claim that Britain had nothing to do with and received no influences whatsoever from the ancient Greek civilization.

In some American universities it is taught that Western civilization has its roots in Africa. It is also taught that the Greek Goddess Athena and philosopher Socrates were coloured people and many other such oddities. It is important that Greek scholars continue to study the influence of the ancient Greek civilization on the other countries. Therefore, it is important that the Greek state and private funding is provided for granting scholarships to post-graduate students in order to study the movement of Greeks in the ancient world. This will facilitate and accelerate the discovery of relevant historical facts.

BIBLIOGRAPHY

Aileen F. South West England *1964*

Barber R.L.N. Cyclades *1994*

Κωνσταντινίδης E.A. Η Οικουμενική Διάσταση της Ελληνικής Γλώσσας *Ελλάς 2001*

Barry Cunliffe Πυθέας ο΄Ελληνας *Εκδόσεις Γκοβόστη 2003*

Bass G.F. Oldest Known Shipwreck *National Geographic Vol 172/ 6 1987pp 692-733*

Boardman J. The Greeks Overseas *London 1980*

Burn R.A. A Travelers History of Greece *1965*

Carl W.B. Troy *1966*

Catling W.H. Late Minoan Vases and Bronzes in Oxford *1968*

Charles F.P. Roy A.M. Ore Deposits *1963*

Colin Wilson - Rand Flem The Atlantis Blueprint *USA 2001*

Donald H. The Phoenicians *1962*

Galanopoulos and Bacon Atlantis *1969*

Glotz G. Aegean Civilization *1941*

Field L.G. The Growth of Civilization *1966*

Homer L. T. Near Eastern, Mediterranean and European Chronology *1967*

Hamlyn P. The River People of Long Ago *1963*

Institution of Mining and Metallurgy Bulletin No 777 *August 1971*

Ιωαννίδη Παντελή Κ. Η Άγνωστη Προϊστορία των Ελλήνων *1966*

Λαζός Χρήστος Δ. Το ταξίδι του Πυθέα στην Άγνωστη Θούλη, *Ελλάδα 1996*

Leonard R.P. Mycenaeans and Minoans *1965*

Leonard C.W. The Sumerians *1965*

Lord W.T. The Mycenaeans *1966*

Luce V.J. The End of Altantis *1969*

Mike Pitts Hengeworld *Great Britain 2001*

Μπουρδάκου Ε.Λ. Ηρακλής *Ελλάς 2003*

Nors S. Josephon Ένας Αρχαϊκός Ελληνικός Πολιτισμός στη Νήσο του Πάσχα *Translation to Greek 2003.*

Nors S. Josephon Greek Linguistic Elements in the Polynesian Languages *Heidelberg 1987*

Πέδρο Ολάγια Μυθολογικός Άτλας της Ελλάδας *Εκδόσεις Road 2001, Ελλάδα.*

Reynold H. Minoan and Mycenaean Art *1967,1981*

Rivet F.L.A. and Colin S. The place Names of Roman Britain *New Jersey 1979*

Rob R. Stone Circles *USA 1999*

Rodney C. The Making of Stonehenge *London New York 1993*

Singlair H. The Minoans *1971*

Tylcote F.R. Metallurgy in Anchaeology *1962*

Tacitus On Britain and Germany *Penguin Books 1995*

Apollodorus	Books
Aristotele	Meteorologica
Diodorus Siculus	Books
Herodotus	Books
Homer	Iliad Odyssey
Plato	Critias Timaeus
Pliny	Natural History
Polyvius	History
Strabo	Geography

Index

A

B

C

D

I

J

K

L

M

N

O

P

R

S

T

U

V

W

Z